Level E

Vocabulary for Listening, Speaking, Reading, and Writing

Author

Jerry Zutell, Ph.D.
The Ohio State University

Credits: Located on last page of book

ISBN: 0-7367-2449-4

Copyright © 2005 Zaner-Bloser, Inc.

Zaner-Bloser, Inc., P.O. Box 16764, Columbus, Ohio 43216-6764 (1-800-421-3018)
www.zaner-bloser.com

A ZB Language Arts Program

Contents

4 UNIT THEME
Communication   72

5 UNIT THEME
Measurement   94

6 UNIT THEME Work and Money 116

7 UNIT THEME Language and Writing 138

8 UNIT THEME Legal Matters 160

**9 UNIT THEME
Good and Bad   182**

Context Clues

A Restaurant Review:

Aunt Edna's Kitchen

Eating well sometimes means dining in a restaurant. How do diners choose a restaurant? One way is by reading about the experience of an expert who has visited the restaurant.

Downtown Springwood has a new restaurant, Aunt Edna's Kitchen, and it's already a popular spot. I visited on a Saturday evening, and the place was filled with diners of all ages. The space is large and airy, and dividers with plantings keep the noise level under control. The menu includes fish, meat, and poultry dishes. There are also **vegetarian** dishes prepared with products grown on local farms. The salad greens tasted so fresh that I could almost believe I had just plucked them from a garden. The dressing was light and not oily, and I sniffed a pleasant ginger **aroma**.

There were many **appetizers** to choose from, but I sampled two. The fried shrimp was crunchy and moist. I nibbled, trying not to **devour** them all. The potato rolls arrived still steaming and tasted heavenly. I limited myself to one so that I would still have room for the main dish.

For the **entrée,** I selected grilled chicken and pasta. The **abundant** serving was more than enough for one person. I **savored** the lemon and pepper flavors in the chicken. The pasta was wide, **flavorful** noodles that were neither too soft nor too firm, but cooked just right.

The dessert offerings included thick chocolate cake, homemade ice cream and pudding, and a **nutritious** fruit plate for those who prefer healthful fare.

The **chef** is Roland Miller. He explained that he is also the owner of Aunt Edna's Kitchen and has been a baker and a restaurant manager. His restaurant is named after his aunt, an imaginative cook, whose recipes he still uses.

With its reasonable prices and polite and fast service, Aunt Edna's Kitchen is sure to become a Springwood favorite.

Context Clues Strategy

Look for What Kind of Thing the Word Is

EXAMPLE: You may add flavor with mustard, sauce, relish, or another *condiment*.

CLUE: The words *mustard, sauce,* and *relish* all tell what kind of thing a *condiment* is.

Using the context is a good way to understand the meaning of a new word. Here is one strategy for using context clues.

Read the sentence with the unknown word and some of the sentences around it.

The chef is Roland Miller. He explained that he is also the owner of Aunt Edna's Kitchen and has been a baker and a restaurant manager.

Look for context clues. **What Kind of Thing** seems to be named?

The words *owner, baker, restaurant manager,* and *cook* are clues that tell what kind of thing, or person, a *chef* is.

Think about the context clues and other information you may already know.

The owner of a restaurant is sometimes the chief cook.

Predict a meaning for the word.

The word *chef* probably means "the chief cook in a restaurant."

Check the Word Wisdom Dictionary to be sure of the meaning.

A *chef* is "the head cook in a place that serves food."

Unlock the Meanings

Practice the Strategy One of the boldfaced words from the restaurant review on page 6 appears below. Use the context clues strategy on page 7 to figure out the meaning of the word.

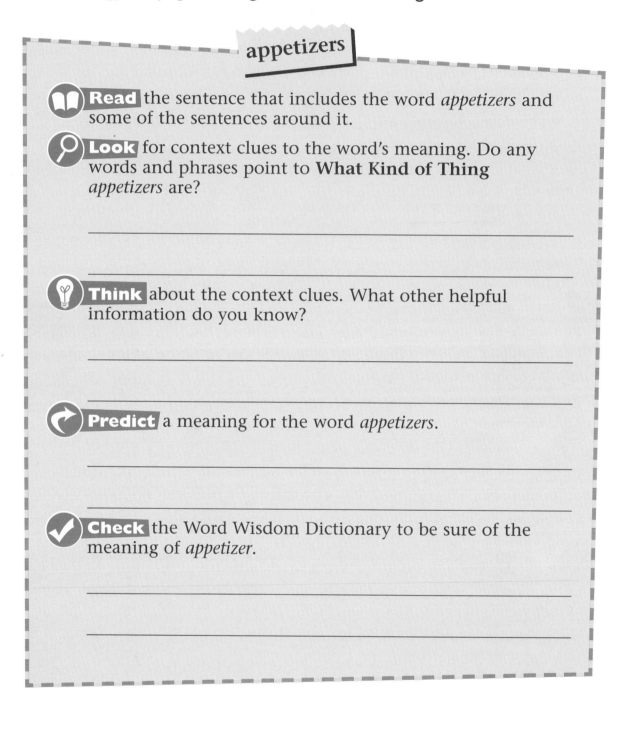

appetizers

Read the sentence that includes the word *appetizers* and some of the sentences around it.

Look for context clues to the word's meaning. Do any words and phrases point to **What Kind of Thing** *appetizers* are?

_____

_____

Think about the context clues. What other helpful information do you know?

_____

_____

Predict a meaning for the word *appetizers*.

_____

_____

Check the Word Wisdom Dictionary to be sure of the meaning of *appetizer*.

_____

_____

vegetarian
aroma
✔appetizer
devour
entrée
abundant
savor
flavorful
nutritious
✔chef

Use Context Clues You have been introduced to two vocabulary words from the restaurant review on page 6. Those words are checked off in the Word List on this page. Under "Vocabulary Word" below, write the other eight words from the Word List. Predict a meaning for each word under "Your Prediction." Then check the words in the Word Wisdom Dictionary. Write the definition under "Dictionary Says."

	Vocabulary Word	Your Prediction	Dictionary Says
1			
2			
3			
4			
5			
6			
7			
8			

Process the Meanings

WORD LIST

vegetarian

aroma

appetizer

devour

entrée

abundant

savor

flavorful

nutritious

chef

Use the Words Correctly in Writing Rewrite each sentence in your own words. Include the word in parentheses.

1 Some sandwiches have vegetables but no meat. (vegetarian)

_____

2 People passing by the bakery can breathe in the smell. (aroma)

_____

3 The guests enjoyed the dip before the meal. (appetizer)

_____

4 Chew slowly, and don't gobble up your food. (devour)

_____

5 A large salad can serve as a whole, filling meal. (entrée)

_____

6 People can celebrate a harvest with a feast. (abundant)

_____

7 "I enjoy every bite," said the diner. (savor)

_____

8 Spices can make a dish very tasty. (flavorful)

_____

9 Junk food tastes good, but it's bad for you. (nutritious)

_____

10 The pastry baker was trained in France. (chef)

_____

Apply What You've Learned

Understand Word Meanings Answer each question **Yes** or **No**. Then write a brief reason for your choice. Include both boldfaced words in your answer.

1 Is **flavorful** food always **abundant**?

_____

_____

2 Can a **vegetarian** soup be **nutritious**?

_____

_____

3 Is it possible to **savor** an **entrée**?

_____

_____

4 Can a **devour** be an **appetizer**?

_____

_____

Give Examples List one or two examples for each item.

5 things that a **chef** does

_____

7 things that have an **aroma**

_____

6 **appetizers** you have eaten

_____

8 **nutritious** snacks

_____

Write It! Write a paragraph describing your favorite food. Use as many of the words from the Word List on page 10 as you can.

Latin Roots

for Word Wisdom

Plants or Animals:
Diets in the Wild

Do you know someone who is a vegetarian? If you do, you know that vegetarians eat mostly plant products. They do not eat animal meat. On the other hand, there are also a lot of people who eat a diet rich in meaty foods. Animals in the wild have different kinds of diets, too.

In nature, a vegetarian animal is called a **herbivore**. An animal that eats mostly meat is called a **carnivore**. Lions are great examples of carnivores. Some people believe lions have an **insatiable** desire to kill prey and eat. But this is not exactly true. It is true that lions have a **voracious** appetite when food is available. But once they have been **satiated,** or satisfied, by a large meal, lions can go for days without eating. They will hunt only when they become hungry again.

When the members of a pride catch the scent of a **savory** meal, they all prepare for a feast. After a kill, lions eat in a certain order. Males eat first. When they are finished, females move in and fight

each other to get a bite. Finally, when the adults have eaten, the young cubs get the chance to **nourish** their growing bodies. Usually only a few bones of the prey are left behind and, perhaps, a puddle of blood that has **saturated** the dirt.

Eating is a different process for herbivores than it is for most carnivores. Herbivores need to eat a large quantity of food. Elephants are herbivores. An elephant will spend most of its day—every day—eating. In fact, an adult elephant can eat between two and three hundred pounds of food a day! A large variety of food also helps them get all the **nutrients** their bodies need. They eat leaves, twigs, fruits, flowers, and grasses, among other things. We humans prefer to eat food with a lot of flavor. But elephants will eat even **insipid** foods, such as tree bark and plant roots.

Although humans are a part of the animal kingdom, we don't eat exactly like the carnivores and herbivores of the wild. For one thing, we're a bit more finicky about what we eat!

Practice the Context Clues Strategy Here is one of the boldfaced words from the essay on page 12. Use the context clues strategy you learned in Part 1 on page 7 to figure out the meaning of this word.

saturated

Read the sentence that uses the word *saturated*. Read some of the sentences around the word.

Look for context clues. What words tell **What Kind of Thing the Word Is**?

_____

_____

_____

Think about the context clues. What other helpful information do you know?

_____

_____

Predict a meaning for the word *saturate*.

_____

_____

_____

Check your Word Wisdom Dictionary to be sure of the meaning of the word *saturate*. Which of the meanings fits the context?

_____

_____

_____

Many English words have a main part called a root. Knowing the meaning of the root can help you figure out the meaning of a new word. Each Latin root below has something to do with food.

Latin Root: **sap, sav, sip**
meaning: to taste
English word: *savor*
meaning: to taste with enjoyment

Latin Root: **nour, nur, nut**
meaning: to feed
English word: *nutritious*
meaning: nourishing

Latin Root: **vor**
meaning: to swallow
English word: *devour*
meaning: to eat greedily

Latin Root: **sat**
meaning: enough
English word: *satiate*
meaning: to satisfy a hunger or desire

Sort by Roots Find the Latin roots you just learned in the Word List. Write each word in the correct section.

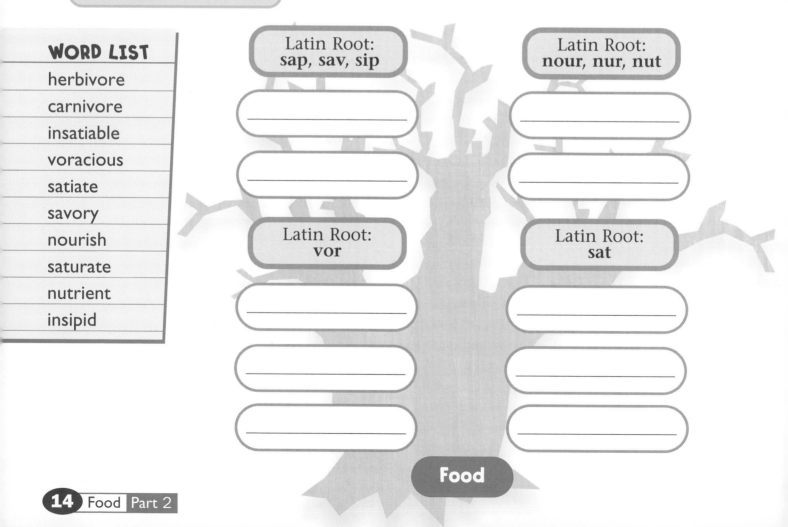

WORD LIST
- herbivore
- carnivore
- insatiable
- voracious
- satiate
- savory
- nourish
- saturate
- nutrient
- insipid

Latin Root: sap, sav, sip

Latin Root: nour, nur, nut

Latin Root: vor

Latin Root: sat

Food

Prefix	Meaning
in-	not

Example

in- (not) + sat (enough) + able (adj.) = insatiable

Use Roots and Prefixes Circle any roots and prefixes that you find in the boldfaced words. Use roots, prefixes, and context clues to write the meaning of each word. Check your definitions in the Word Wisdom Dictionary.

1 Vitamin C is a **nutrient** found in oranges.

_____

2 The heavy rain **saturated** the ground.

_____

3 Deer are **herbivores**, so we put a fence around our vegetable garden.

_____

4 After her hike, Emma had a **voracious** appetite.

_____

5 The chef added spices to give flavor to the **insipid** soup.

_____

6 **Nourish** your body by eating different kinds of food.

_____

7 Juan has an **insatiable** interest in comets, so he reads about them.

_____

8 Mia couldn't wait to eat the **savory** meal her grandpa cooked.

_____

9 Only some dinosaurs were **carnivores**. Many ate plants.

_____

10 Mom's need for adventure was **satiated** by a trip down the Green River.

_____

Process the Meanings

WORD LIST

- herbivore
- carnivore
- insatiable
- voracious
- satiate
- savory
- nourish
- saturate
- nutrient
- insipid

Choose the Correct Word Write the correct word from the Word List to complete each sentence. You may have to add an ending. Then underline the words in the sentence that helped you make your choice.

1 A lion is a _____ because it eats zebras.

2 Drinking a jug of water should _____ Mac's thirst.

3 Customers refused to eat the _____ stew because it had no flavor.

4 After football practice, Deon had a _____ appetite.

5 After I wiped up the spilled soda, my sponge was completely _____.

6 Vitamins and minerals are important _____.

Find the Antonyms After each word below, write a word from the Word List that is opposite or nearly opposite in meaning.

Word	Antonym
7 insipid	_____
8 starve	_____
9 satisfied	_____
10 carnivore	_____

Apply What You've Learned

Demonstrate Word Knowledge Write a sentence that answers each question.

1 What kinds of foods would a **savory** meal contain?

_____

2 If you had an **insatiable** interest in movies, what might you do?

_____

3 What are some **nutrients** in a good breakfast?

_____

4 What are some things that **herbivores** might eat?

_____

5 What are some things that a **carnivore** might eat?

_____

6 If the air were **saturated** with moisture, what could happen?

_____

7 When might you have a **voracious** appetite?

_____

8 Where could an athlete go to **satiate** her need to exercise?

_____

9 How would **insipid** food taste?

_____

10 How can you **nourish** your body?

_____

Speak It! Give a short talk on the importance of eating well. Use words from the Part 2 Word List.

PART 3 Reference Skills

for Word Wisdom

You Want Me to Eat What?

Foods Around the World

Imagine that you are on a fun vacation in England. You go to a nice restaurant for dinner, but the menu is filled with foods you do not recognize. You order "black pudding" because at least you know what pudding is. When it arrives at your table, you realize that black pudding is sausage made from the blood of a pig! Yuck!

Food preferences are different all over the world. What we think is **disgusting** to eat, people in other countries might enjoy. Let's take a look at some of the foods eaten in other parts of the world.

In the Philippines, there is a traditional meal called "chocolate pork" stew, or *diniguan*. Don't let the word *chocolate* fool you, though. It might sound sweet, but it is not a **confection**. It is a **concoction** of pig blood mixed with pig parts, such as the head, liver, and heart. While you and I might find this dish **distasteful**, it is very popular in that country. The Philippines is also home to *baalut,* a meal that begins with a chicken egg. This might sound

palatable so far, but there is more to the meal. The egg is buried in the ground for a few weeks. Then the **putrid** egg is dug up and eaten. Have you ever smelled a rotten egg? How would you like to eat one?

In Japan, one popular **delicacy** is the puffer fish, or *fugu*. This poisonous fish must be prepared just right. Otherwise, the person eating it could be paralyzed or die. In fact, experts estimate that 300 people a year die from eating *fugu*.

A **sumptuous** meal in China is monkey brains. Some people in Tibet enjoy drinking yak milk that is **rancid** instead of being fresh and unspoiled. Certain tribes in Africa drink the fresh blood of the animals they kill. And down under in Australia, kangaroo meat is becoming more and more popular.

People in some parts of the world also enjoy eating insects. If you found worms in your food, you would probably think it was **contaminated** and throw it away. But in Korea, people eat worms. And people in many countries eat grasshoppers and crickets. Some people even eat chocolate-covered ants. And you thought Brussels sprouts were gross!

Practice the Context Clues Strategy Here is one of the boldfaced words from the essay on page 18. Use the context clues strategy you learned in Part 1 on page 7 to figure out the meaning of this word.

confection

Read the sentence that uses the word *confection*. Read some of the sentences around the word.

Look for context clues. What words tell you **What Kind of Thing the Word Is?**

_____

_____

_____

Think about the context clues. What other helpful information do you know?

_____

_____

_____

Predict a meaning for the word *confection*.

_____

_____

_____

Check your Word Wisdom Dictionary to be sure of the meaning of the word *confection*. Write the definition here.

_____

_____

_____

The Dictionary Words in the dictionary are listed in alphabetical order. The dictionary is divided into sections, with tabs or indents to show where the sections are located.

When looking up a word's meaning in a dictionary, find the section that contains all the words that begin with the same letter as the word you are looking up. Then, look for words that have the same two or three letters after the first letter as the word you're looking for.

Finding Words in the Dictionary Use a dictionary to look up the words *rancid, concoction, delicacy, palatable,* and *contaminate* from the Word List on page 21. Place each word in the chart below in alphabetical order. Write the words that appear in the dictionary before and after the vocabulary word.

Vocabulary Word	Word Before Vocabulary Word	Word After Vocabulary Word

Find the Meaning

1. Use context clues.
2. Look for a familiar root, prefix, or suffix.
3. If the context or a word part doesn't help, check the dictionary.

Define the Words Follow the steps to write the meaning of the boldfaced words. Write 1, 2, or 3 to show which steps you used.

WORD LIST
disgusting
confection
concoction
distasteful
palatable
putrid
delicacy
sumptuous
rancid
contaminate

1 The **concoction** was made with walnuts and cream cheese.

_____

2 Ten chefs prepared the **sumptuous** feast for the king's wedding.

_____

3 After a week, the milk became **rancid** and unfit to drink.

_____

4 Fish eggs are a **delicacy** served on special occasions.

_____

5 Uncle Tony adjusted the recipe until the sauce was **palatable**.

_____

6 The lovely **confection** was decorated with icing and flowers.

_____

7 After lying on the counter all night, the fish became **putrid**.

_____

8 The children thought the green noodles looked **disgusting**.

_____

9 Leaking oil and chemicals can **contaminate** drinking water.

_____

10 Chopping onions can be a **distasteful** chore.

_____

Process the Meanings

WORD LIST

disgusting

confection

concoction

distasteful

palatable

putrid

delicacy

sumptuous

rancid

contaminate

Find the Synonyms Choose a word from the Word List that matches each synonym below, and write the word on the line.

1 unpleasant _____

2 pollute _____

3 magnificent _____

4 rotten _____

5 sickening _____

Complete the Meanings Write the word that best completes each sentence.

6 A **confection** tastes _____.

    sour   sweet   spicy

7 Food that is **palatable** is _____.

    bitter   chunky   tasty

8 If butter became **rancid**, it would be

_____.

    spoiled   fresh   melted

9 A **concoction** is a _____.

    mixture   cake   meal

10 If a food is called a **delicacy**, it is very

_____.

    plain   inexpensive   special

Apply What You've Learned

Demonstrate Word Knowledge Circle the letter of the item that correctly completes the sentence or answers the question.

1 To make a **confection**, you would use
   a. sugar   b. garlic

2 Which is *not* a **delicacy**?
   a. bread   b. lobster

3 If food in the refrigerator is **rancid**, you should
   a. eat it   b. throw it away

4 To make a **concoction**, you would
   a. preheat the oven   b. mix together several ingredients

5 Where might you eat a **sumptuous** meal?
   a. at a fancy restaurant   b. at a fast-food chain

6 When something is **contaminated**, it is not
   a. pure   b. helpful

7 A **distasteful** experience would be
   a. disagreeable   b. fun

8 Fruit that is **putrid** is probably
   a. just picked   b. quite old

9 How would a **palatable** steak taste?
   a. too tough   b. good enough to eat

10 If your lunch looked **disgusting**, you would
   a. not want to eat it   b. ask for more

Write It! Write a humorous short story describing a meal you would not want to eat. To get ideas, look through the reading selections on pages 6, 12, and 18. What foods sound disgusting to you? What kind of concoctions would you never eat? Use as many words from the Word List on page 22 as you can.

Review

for Word Wisdom

Categorize the Words Choose words from the Word List to write in each column of the chart. The number in each column heading tells you how many words to list.

WORD LIST

- vegetarian
- aroma
- appetizer
- devour
- entrée
- abundant
- savor
- flavorful
- nutritious
- chef
- herbivore
- carnivore
- insatiable
- voracious
- satiate
- savory
- nourish
- saturate
- nutrient
- insipid
- disgusting
- confection
- concoction
- distasteful
- palatable
- putrid
- delicacy
- sumptuous
- rancid
- contaminate

Words with the Latin root *nur/nut/nour* meaning "to feed" ③	Words with the Latin root *sat* meaning "enough" ③	Words that describe rotten or bad-tasting food ④

Choose the Correct Word Read the sentence and the two words in parentheses. Circle the word that completes the sentence correctly.

1 A ____ may prepare a feast. (chef, carnivore)

2 A big meal sometimes begins with a(n) ____. (confection, appetizer)

3 A ____ often costs more than other foods. (nutrient, delicacy)

4 The delicious ____ was candy made with honey. (confection, entrée)

5 Tasty food is ____. (flavorful, saturated)

Decide and Explain Decide whether each statement is true or false, and circle **T** or **F**. Then write your reason on the lines.

6 Grazing animals, such as cattle, are **herbivores**. T F

_____

7 A jelly-marshmallow-and-banana sandwich is an example of a **concoction**. T F

_____

8 Baking bread can fill a kitchen with an **aroma**. T F

_____

9 A **vegetarian** meal can be made with beef, chicken, or fish. T F

_____

10 An example of an **insipid** food is a spicy sauce. T F

_____

Taking Vocabulary Tests

Always read the directions first. Pay attention to any words that are in capital letters or special type. Reread to make sure you understand what you are expected to do. Repeat the directions in your own words. Look at these three examples:

1. Fill in the circle of the word that means the OPPOSITE of the underlined word.

2. Fill in the circle by the answer that BEST completes the sentence.

3. Fill in the circle by the answer that has the **same** or **almost the same** meaning as the boldfaced word.

Practice Test Fill in the circle of the word that has the **same** or **almost the same** meaning as the boldfaced word.

1 a **voracious** eater
- ○ quiet
- ○ noisy
- ○ greedy
- ○ picky

2 a **savory** stew
- ○ tasty
- ○ smelly
- ○ large
- ○ hot

3 a **sumptuous** meal
- ○ prepared
- ○ splendid
- ○ spicy
- ○ spoiled

4 an **abundant** portion
- ○ large
- ○ eaten
- ○ available
- ○ undersized

5 food that is **palatable**
- ○ sweet
- ○ unusual
- ○ tasteless
- ○ eatable

6 to **devour** dessert
- ○ gobble
- ○ nibble
- ○ refuse
- ○ prepare

7 a sweet **aroma**
- ○ pastry
- ○ taste
- ○ smell
- ○ ingredient

8 a hungry **carnivore**
- ○ rabbit
- ○ meat eater
- ○ diner
- ○ mind

9 a delicious **entrée**
- ○ snack
- ○ dessert
- ○ main dish
- ○ soup

10 **savor** good food
- ○ keep
- ○ appreciate
- ○ cook
- ○ gulp

Build New Words

Use Suffixes Some suffixes turn words into nouns. Three noun-making suffixes are *-ion, -ness,* and *-ment.* Use these suffixes to make nouns from *saturate, contaminate, nourish, sumptuous,* and *satiate.* Make any needed spelling changes, and check spellings and meanings in your Word Wisdom Dictionary. Then write a phrase to show the meaning of the new word. An example is shown in the first row of the chart.

Word	+ Suffix	= New Word	Phrase
saturate	-ion	saturation	saturation of pancakes with syrup
contaminate			
nourish			
sumptuous			
satiate			

Speak It! Work with a partner to role-play an interview between a talk show host and a famous chef. Include as many words as you can from this unit.

PART 1

Context Clues

for Word Wisdom

The Olympic Games:

An Amazing Jump

The motto of the Olympic Games is a Latin phrase that means "Faster, Higher, Stronger." The motto fits because Olympic athletes often set records as they compete. One Olympic athlete set a new record with an amazing jump.

Every four years, the world's best athletes gather for the summer Olympic Games. The track-and-field events include the 100-meter dash. The winner of this **sprint** is called the fastest man or woman in the world. The winner of another event, the **marathon,** runs more than 26 miles in just over two hours. What a test of **endurance**! Some track-and-field events can make viewers gasp in awe. One of them is the long jump.

The long jump only looks simple. The athlete begins at one end of a runway and **accelerates** smoothly, step by step. Reaching top speed at the takeoff board, the athlete pushes off with one foot and jumps into a sandy pit. Long jumpers need just the right speed and number of steps. They must have the proper foot position and **traction,** or grip, on the takeoff board. And they must control leg, arm, and body movements to avoid **flailing** uselessly and losing balance in the air.

In 1968, the American long jumper Bob Beamon was competing in the Olympic Games in Mexico City. He was not expected to win the event because his jumps were sometimes too short. Experts thought that even if he did his best, he would still **trail** the world-record holders competing against him. At the time, the record for the long jump was just under 27 feet, 5 inches.

Beamon's turn came. He **hurtled** down the runway like a horse at full gallop. He stepped on the takeoff board and leaped. He landed almost beyond the sand pit! The awestruck crowd roared. Beamon's jump was measured at 29 feet, 2$\frac{1}{2}$ inches. He had broken the world record by nearly two feet! He almost couldn't believe what he had done and **collapsed** on the ground.

Bob Beamon **retained** the record for 23 years. His Olympic jump has been called one of the greatest athletic achievements ever.

Context Clues Strategy

Look for How Something Is Done

EXAMPLE: The gymnast *catapulted* powerfully into the air.

CLUE: The word *powerfully* describes the word *catapulted*. It tells how catapulting is done.

Here are the steps for using this context clues strategy to figure out the meaning of *accelerates*.

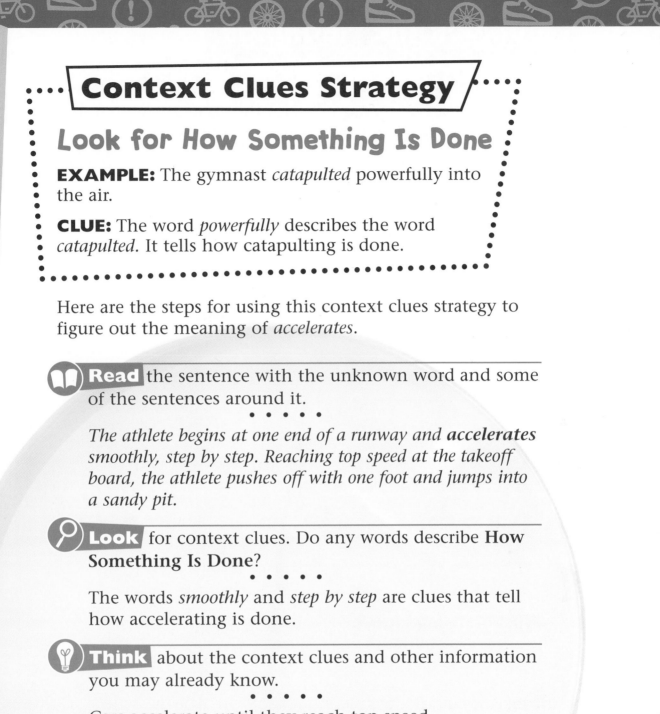

Read the sentence with the unknown word and some of the sentences around it.

*The athlete begins at one end of a runway and **accelerates** smoothly, step by step. Reaching top speed at the takeoff board, the athlete pushes off with one foot and jumps into a sandy pit.*

Look for context clues. Do any words describe **How Something Is Done?**

The words *smoothly* and *step by step* are clues that tell how accelerating is done.

Think about the context clues and other information you may already know.

Cars accelerate until they reach top speed.

Predict a meaning for the word.

The word *accelerates* probably means "goes faster."

Check your Word Wisdom Dictionary to be sure of the meaning. Decide which meaning fits the context.

Accelerates means "goes faster."

Practice the Strategy   The word below is from the article about Bob Beamon on page 28. Use the context clues strategy on page 29 to figure out the meaning of the word.

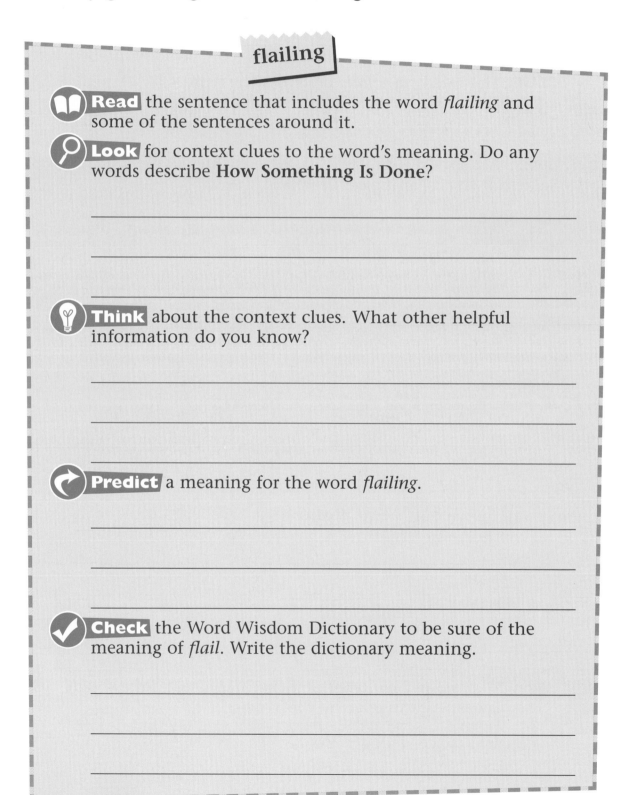

flailing

Read the sentence that includes the word *flailing* and some of the sentences around it.

Look for context clues to the word's meaning. Do any words describe **How Something Is Done?**

_____

_____

Think about the context clues. What other helpful information do you know?

_____

_____

_____

Predict a meaning for the word *flailing*.

_____

_____

_____

Check the Word Wisdom Dictionary to be sure of the meaning of *flail*. Write the dictionary meaning.

_____

_____

_____

sprint
marathon
endurance
✔ accelerate
traction
✔ flail
trail
hurtle
collapse
retain

Use Context Clues You have been introduced to two vocabulary words from the article about the amazing long jump. Those words are checked off in the Word List. Under "Vocabulary Word" below, write the other eight words from the Word List. Use context clues to predict a meaning for each word under "Your Prediction." Then check the meanings in the Word Wisdom Dictionary. Write the definition under "Dictionary Says."

	Vocabulary Word	Your Prediction	Dictionary Says
1			
2			
3			
4			
5			
6			
7			
8			

Process the Meanings

WORD LIST

- sprint
- marathon
- endurance
- accelerate
- traction
- flail
- trail
- hurtle
- collapse
- retain

Find the Synonyms   Write the word from the Word List that is a synonym for the boldfaced word.

1 A poorly built bridge may **tumble**. _____

2 The swimmer began to **thrash**. _____

3 The shortest footrace is the **dash**. _____

4 The **grip** of these tires is strong. _____

5 I'm late. Make the car **quicken**. _____

Use the Words Correctly in Writing   Rewrite each sentence to include the word in parentheses.

6 My team scored, so it will hold onto its lead. (retain)

_____

_____

7 All the runners lag behind the three leaders. (trail)

_____

_____

8 Trains speed noisily through the tunnel. (hurtle)

_____

9 Running a race that is just over 26 miles requires months of training. (marathon)

_____

_____

10 Athletes develop their ability to keep going. (endurance)

_____

Apply What You've Learned

Explain the Differences Answer the questions.

1 Why would you **hurtle**, not jog, if you wanted to win a race?

_____

2 What's different about a car that **accelerates** and one that stops?

_____

3 Would you rather have your favorite team **trail** or tie?

_____

4 Is it better for dancers to **flail** their arms or to swing them?

_____

5 What is the difference between a **marathon** and a **sprint**?

_____

Tell Why Complete each sentence.

6 Soccer players need **endurance** _____

7 A person may **collapse** on a hot day _____

8 Fans **retain** hope when their team is losing _____

_____

9 Running shoes have good **traction** _____

10 A **sprint** may last a few seconds because _____

_____

Write It! Imagine running a marathon. Write a paragraph to describe the experience. Use as many vocabulary words from Part 1 as you can.

PART 2

Latin Roots

for Word Wisdom

Horse Heroes:

The Sport of Horse Racing

There are some people who think of racehorses as professional athletes—they are strong, powerful, and well trained. But what is so interesting about this popular sport?

Have you ever watched a horse race? If you have, you know that horse racing **attracts** many fans. Thousands of people attend the major horse races. Even more people watch them on TV. In fact, horse racing is one of the oldest sports in history.

Most of the major races take place among thoroughbred horses. A thoroughbred is a breed of horse. They are usually strong, fast, and **agile** animals. A horse's parents and grandparents are very important. If a horse's parent was a good racer, then that horse will likely be a good racer, too. Some racehorses are even **extracted** from the sport in order for them to breed new racehorses.

At a race, horses are led into their own stalls, or enclosed areas. They are **detained** here until the race begins. The stall is just big enough for the horse to fit. It is important to keep the horse calm in the stall. If it becomes **agitated**, the horse might have a difficult start to the race. At the front of each stall is a gate where the horses line up. When the official **activates** a button, the gates open. The horses burst onto the track.

Some races, such as the famous Kentucky Derby, can **contain** twenty horses. Each horse has a jockey, or rider. He or she helps the horse **maintain** a certain speed during the race. A jockey helps the horse **react** to the movement of the other horses. Sometimes a pack of several horses will **contract** and run very near each other. This is common when horses run around bends in the track. A jockey must always guide the horse properly.

Winners of the major races become sports heroes. Horse racing in the U.S. has an honor called the Triple Crown. A horse that wins the Triple Crown has won the three major horse races—the Kentucky Derby, the Preakness Stakes, and the Belmont Stakes—in the same year. A few Triple Crown winners are the horses Secretariat, Citation, and War Admiral. Among race fans, these three horses are remembered as heroes.

Practice the Context Clues Strategy Here is one of the boldfaced words from the essay on page 34. Use the context clues strategy you learned in Part 1 on page 29 to figure out the meaning of this word.

contract

Read the sentence that uses the word *contract*. Read some of the sentences around the word.

Look for context clues. Do any words describe **How Something Is Done?**

_____

_____

_____

Think about the context clues. What other helpful information do you know?

_____

_____

_____

Predict a meaning for the word *contract*.

_____

_____

_____

Check your Word Wisdom Dictionary to be sure of the meaning of the word *contract*. Which meaning for *contract* fits the context?

_____

_____

_____

Unlock the Meanings

The main part of most English words is called the root. In this lesson you will learn three Latin roots. Each one has something to do with movement.

Latin Root: **act, agi**
meaning: to act, to do
English word: *actor*
meaning: a person who acts

Latin Root: **tract**
meaning: to pull, to draw
English word: *traction*
meaning: the grip needed to pull an object

Latin Root: **ten, tin, tain**
meaning: to hold
English word: *retain*
meaning: to keep or hold

WORD LIST

- attract
- agile
- extract
- detain
- agitate
- activate
- contain
- maintain
- react
- contract

Sort by Roots Find these roots in the words from the Word List on this page. Then write each word in the correct column. Think of other words you know that come from the same Latin roots. Write each one in the correct column.

Movement

Latin Root: **act, agi**

Latin Root: **tract**

Latin Root: **ten, tin, tain**

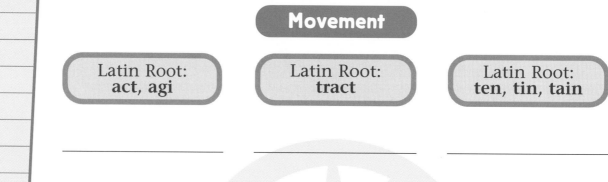

Prefix	Meaning
ad-, at-	toward, to
de-	from

Example

at- (toward) + **tract** (pull) = **attract**

Use Roots and Prefixes Circle any roots and prefixes you find in each boldfaced word. Use context clues, roots, and prefixes to write the meaning of each word. Check your definitions in the dictionary.

1 The great beauty of the Grand Canyon **attracts** many tourists.

_____

2 After much practice, the once clumsy boy became an **agile** gymnast.

_____

3 Heavy traffic on the freeway **detained** us for nearly an hour.

_____

4 Since some foods **contract** when cold, they become smaller if frozen.

_____

5 A baby might **react** to a loud noise, such as thunder, by crying.

_____

6 You can **maintain** your garden by watering and weeding it regularly.

_____

7 Dad used pointy tweezers to **extract** the splinter from my finger.

_____

8 The robot won't move until you **activate** it by turning the switch.

_____

9 Newspapers often **contain** articles about government.

_____

10 Strong wind can **agitate** the water in a lake.

_____

WORD LIST

- attract
- agile
- extract
- detain
- agitate
- activate
- contain
- maintain
- react
- contract

Choose the Correct Meaning For each phrase below, circle the letter of the item that gives the best meaning for the boldfaced word.

1 to **maintain** good grades in school
- a. keep up
- b. try to get
- c. want to earn

2 **reacted** to an angry comment
- a. added
- b. connected
- c. responded

3 always **attracts** dust
- a. gives off
- b. creates
- c. pulls toward itself

4 **contains** many ingredients
- a. mixes together
- b. has in it
- c. locates

5 was **detained** at the airport
- a. delayed
- b. confused
- c. sleeping

6 will **activate** the rocket launch
- a. quickly stop
- b. set in motion
- c. command

Find the Antonyms Write the word from the Word List that is opposite in meaning to each word or phrase below.

7 calm down _____

8 insert _____

9 clumsy _____

10 expand _____

Apply What You've Learned

Demonstrate Word Knowledge   Use what you have learned about the boldfaced words to answer the questions.

1 What are some valuable things that can be **extracted** from the earth?

_____

2 If you wanted to **attract** attention, what could you do?

_____

3 How might a person **react** to a fire alarm?

_____

4 What are some ways you can **maintain** a bicycle?

_____

5 When might a teacher become **agitated**?

_____

Check the Meaning   Decide whether the boldfaced word has been used correctly. Write **C** for **Correct** or **I** for **Incorrect**.

_____ **6** Aunt Flora was **detained** and arrived home late.

_____ **7** You can **contract** her at home by calling her on the phone.

_____ **8** The **agile** vase had many chips and cracks.

_____ **9** My suitcase **contains** everything I will need for vacation.

_____ **10** A thief will **activate** the alarm if he opens the door.

Speak It!   Create a script for a radio sports report. Describe an exciting game, or report on an interview with a star player. Use as many vocabulary words from Part 2 as you can.

Reference Skills

for Word Wisdom

A Mountain's Challenge:

High Climbing

You have probably heard of Mount Everest. This mountain is famous for how difficult it is to climb. But why climb mountains in the first place? Many people do it for the challenge.

Mountain climbing is a dangerous sport. The higher one climbs, the more dangerous it becomes. Before one **embarks** on such a journey, he or she must know the basics in climbing and survival skills.

To **navigate** the safest way to the top of a mountain, climbers **exert** an incredible amount of physical effort. On Mount Everest and other popular mountains, there are often several base camps set up to offer climbers a break. Base camps are not found very high up a mountain, so it is wise for climbers to **recline**, rest, and prepare their bodies for the remainder of the climb.

Climbers run into many challenges as they **maneuver** their way up a mountain. They might even encounter dangerous wildlife or have to **wade** across a stream that wets their clothes. They might find themselves **suspended** on the face of a steep rock.

Weather changes are another challenge for mountain climbers. The higher a climber goes, the more difficult the weather is to predict. The temperatures get colder, and the weather gets harsher. There is a danger of frostbite and freezing. Avalanches may also occur. Some climbers carry two-way radios. They use these to **transmit** information to each other or to call for help. They may also warn other climbers to take an alternate route.

Physical problems also challenge climbers. As climbers go higher up a mountain, the air gets thinner. Climbers might find it difficult to breathe. They often carry a supply of canned oxygen.

Climbers must remember that even if they reach the summit, they still have to climb back down the mountain. It might be easy to **dismount** a ladder, but climbing down a mountain takes time and energy. Sometimes a climber will **transfer** some of their gear to another climber before heading back down. This makes their load lighter, giving the climber more energy, although much of the energy comes from the thrill of overcoming the mountain's tough challenge!

Practice the Context Clues Strategy Here is one of the boldfaced words from the essay on page 40. Use the context clues strategy you learned in Part 1 on page 29 to figure out the meaning of this word.

dismount

Read the sentence that uses the word *dismount* and some of the sentences around the word.

Look for context clues. Do any words describe **How Something Is Done**?

_____

_____

_____

Think about the context clues. What other helpful information do you know?

_____

_____

_____

Predict a meaning for the word *dismount*.

_____

_____

_____

Check your Word Wisdom Dictionary to be sure of the meaning of the word *dismount*. Write the definition here.

_____

_____

_____

🔑 Unlock the Meanings

Guide Words Dictionaries provide **guide words** to help you find the entry word you're looking for. Guide words appear at the top of each page. They are the first and the last entry words on that page.

Other entries come alphabetically between the two guide words. By looking at the guide words you can quickly decide if the word you want is on that page.

Use Guide Words Write the word from the Word List on page 43 that would be found on the same dictionary page as each set of guide words below. If none of the words would be on the page, write **none**.

1 solid / temperature _____

2 weekend / yellow _____

3 diamond / display _____

4 quiet / remember _____

5 mechanic / nimble _____

6 transfix / tumble _____

7 dominate / elude _____

8 magnify / molecule _____

9 velocity / wheel _____

10 domain / elate _____

Find the Meaning
1. Use context clues.
2. Look for a familiar root, prefix, or suffix.
3. If the context or a word part doesn't help, check the dictionary.

Define the Words Follow the steps above to write the meaning of each boldfaced word. Write 1, 2, or 3 to show which steps you used.

WORD LIST
embark
navigate
exert
recline
maneuver
wade
suspend
transmit
dismount
transfer

1 After I **dismounted** my horse, I led her to the barn.

_____

2 It is easy to **wade** here because the water is shallow.

_____

3 Mrs. Liang **maneuvered** her skis around rocks and trees.

_____

4 At night, sailors can use the stars to help **navigate** their ships.

_____

5 The electrician tried to **suspend** the light from the ceiling.

_____

6 Our class **embarked** on a new project to help homeless families.

_____

7 Mr. Ortiz uses e-mail to **transmit** messages to his students.

_____

8 The workers had to **exert** themselves to move the boulder.

_____

9 After standing all day, Joe was happy to **recline** on the couch.

_____

10 To get downtown, I had to **transfer** to a second bus.

_____

Process the Meanings

WORD LIST

- embark
- navigate
- exert
- recline
- maneuver
- wade
- suspend
- transmit
- dismount
- transfer

Revise the Sentences   Rewrite each sentence. Replace the underlined words with a word from the Word List. You may need to add an ending to the word you choose.

1 Josh was so tired that he lay down in the hammock.

_____

2 Meg could carefully move her skateboard around corners.

_____

3 Cobwebs were hanging down from the ceiling.

_____

4 Coach Rivers taught us how to get off the parallel bars.

_____

5 On Monday, I will move from Frost School to a new one.

_____

Choose the Correct Word   Write the word from the Word List that completes each sentence.

6 It will take days to _____ through the stack of papers on his desk.

7 My parents will _____ on a trip.

8 I know that if I _____ myself, I can learn to play the flute.

9 The airline pilot used instruments to _____ the plane.

10 She hired a trucking company to _____ the heavy boxes.

Apply What You've Learned

Relate the Meanings   Answer the questions.

1 When have you had to **exert** yourself?

_____

2 What would you need to **suspend** a picture on a wall?

_____

3 Where would you be after **dismounting** a horse?

_____

4 If a chair can **recline**, what can it do?

_____

5 How would you **transmit** a note to your teacher?

_____

Choose the Correct Answer   Circle the best answer.

6 Which is *not* something you would **wade** through?
a. the newspaper   b. a brook   c. a tree

7 Sailors who **navigate** ships could use
a. a clock   b. fuel   c. a compass

8 A driver would **maneuver** a car by
a. steering it   b. fixing it   c. washing it

9 Someone who is **embarking** on a new career is
a. experienced   b. starting out   c. talkative

10 To **transfer** books, a librarian might
a. read them   b. move them   c. recommend them

Write It!   Write directions telling how to get to your playground. Use several Part 3 vocabulary words.

Review

for Word Wisdom

Sort Words by Latin Roots Find the words in the Word List that contain the Latin roots listed below. Write each one in the correct section of the chart.

WORD LIST

- sprint
- marathon
- endurance
- accelerate
- traction
- flail
- trail
- hurtle
- collapse
- retain
- attract
- agile
- extract
- detain
- agitate
- activate
- contain
- maintain
- react
- contract
- embark
- navigate
- exert
- recline
- maneuver
- wade
- suspend
- transmit
- dismount
- transfer

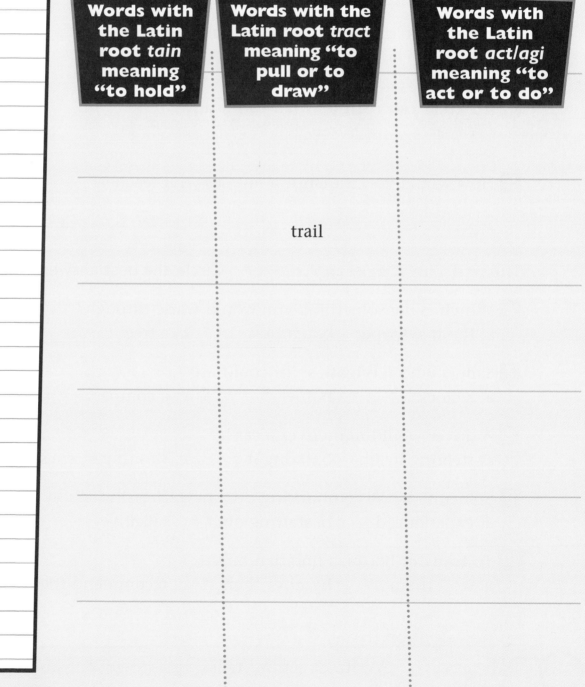

Words with the Latin root *tain* meaning "to hold"	Words with the Latin root *tract* meaning "to pull or to draw"	Words with the Latin root *act/agi* meaning "to act or to do"
	trail	

Check the Meaning Decide whether the boldfaced word has been used correctly. Write **C** for **Correct** or **I** for **Incorrect**. Then write a sentence telling why it is correct or incorrect.

____ **1** A washing machine **agitates** the clothes.

_____

____ **2** People often relax when they **recline**.

_____

____ **3** Six dogs **embarked** and kept the neighbors awake.

_____

____ **4** Please **extract** the seeds from the watermelon.

_____

____ **5** We climbed the steep **dismount**.

_____

____ **6** Student drivers learn how to **maneuver** a car.

_____

Choose the Correct Word Write the word from the Word List that best completes each sentence.

7 The people in the _____ ran for miles.

8 The storm caused roofs to _____.

9 Mountain goats leap and run on steep cliffs, so they must

be _____.

10 If your boots have good _____, you won't slip on the ice.

Taking Vocabulary Tests

Practice Test   Fill in the letter of the answer that best completes the sentence.

1 Please **transmit** the message by ____.
- (A) erasing it
- (B) telephone
- (C) listening
- (D) payment

2 Someone who **hurtles** is always ____.
- (A) in pain
- (B) leaping
- (C) speedy
- (D) ahead

3 A person who **trails** a deer is ____.
- (A) protecting it
- (B) carrying it
- (C) ahead of it
- (D) following it

4 A **sprint** is a ____.
- (A) short race
- (B) kind of first aid
- (C) broken bone
- (D) sports star

5 People may **flail** their ____.
- (A) teeth
- (B) eyebrows
- (C) arms
- (D) eyes

6 A test of **endurance** is usually ____.
- (A) long
- (B) tired
- (C) wise
- (D) early

7 Let's **accelerate** our ____.
- (A) pace
- (B) homework
- (C) trash
- (D) sleep

8 Travelers may **transfer** ____.
- (A) a foreign language
- (B) train tickets
- (C) sights
- (D) new countries

9 My dog **waded** ____.
- (A) inside a bone
- (B) by the vet's office
- (C) across the yard
- (D) into the pond

10 If you **suspend** a plant, you ____.
- (A) destroy it
- (B) hide it
- (C) water it
- (D) hang it

Play with Language

Suffix *-ion* Puzzle Turn each verb below into a noun by adding the suffixes *-ion* or *-ation*. You may need to make other spelling changes, too. Write one letter of the noun on each blank following the word. Some blanks are enclosed in circles.

1 exert — — — — — — — — —

2 activate — — — ◯ — — — —

3 contract — ◯ — — — — — — —

4 navigate — — — ◯ — — —

5 extract — — — — ◯ — — — —

6 transmit — — ◯ — — — — — — —

7 embark — ◯ — — — — — —

8 accelerate — — — ◯ — — — — —

9 attract — — — ◯ — — — —

10 suspend — ◯ — — — — — —

Now unscramble the circled letters to write the answer to this riddle: *What grows bigger and better the more you use it?* One letter has been given.

— — — — — — — — _y_

Speak It! Think of an animal you have seen or read about. It might be a pet, an animal at the zoo, or another creature. Describe how the animal moves when it walks, runs, or swims. Use as many of the words from this Movement unit as you can.

Context Clues

for Word Wisdom

Bird Brains:

Do Birds Have Brain Power?

In some folktales and fables, birds are clever and wise. Are real birds able to think? How can we tell? For a long time scientists have wondered about those questions. Read this article about birds' ability to think.

Scientists who study birds' thinking face a problem. Thinking can't be seen. Trying to **infer** a bird's thoughts is like doing detective work. The clues are in the bird's behaviors. Scientists use the basic **principle,** or idea, that complicated actions take more brainwork than simple ones.

One bird with complicated behaviors is the male bowerbird of Australia. This bird builds a large structure, called a bower, to attract a female. The males decorate the bowers with twigs, leaves, grass, feathers, berries, flowers, and other colorful items. If a female shows up, the male sings and dances to invite her into his showy bower.

But is the male bowerbird really "thinking" as he **methodically** puts together his bower? Is he **conscious** of what he is doing? Or is he unaware of his actions? Bower building might be an **instinct,** like the inborn ability to fly.

One scientist **investigated** ravens, birds famous for their cleverness. He tied one end of a long string to the birds' perch. He hung a piece of meat from the other end of the string. The ravens could not get a grip on the meat. After several tries, they gave up.

However, one raven acted like an **ingenious** inventor. On the perch, the raven pulled up some of the string in its bill and tucked it under one foot. The raven did this until it had pulled up the meat. What does the **outcome** of this test show? The raven seemed to be using **insight,** a thinking skill, to a solve a problem.

Some scientists **propose** that birds are indeed thinkers because they show creativity and problem-solving skills.

Context Clues Strategy

Look for What the Word Is Like

EXAMPLE: Like a picture formed in the mind, an *intention* is a kind of mental activity.

CLUE: The phrase *Like a picture formed in the mind* compares the word *intention* to something familiar.

Here are the steps for using this context clues strategy to figure out the meaning of the word *infer*.

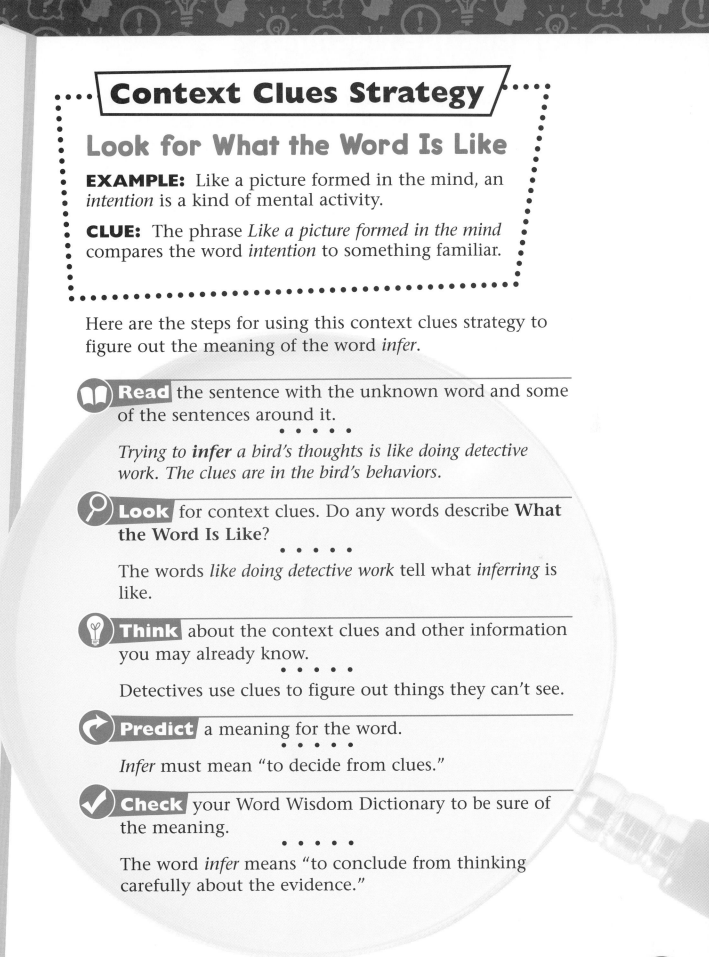

Read the sentence with the unknown word and some of the sentences around it.

*Trying to **infer** a bird's thoughts is like doing detective work. The clues are in the bird's behaviors.*

Look for context clues. Do any words describe **What the Word Is Like?**

The words *like doing detective work* tell what *inferring* is like.

Think about the context clues and other information you may already know.

Detectives use clues to figure out things they can't see.

Predict a meaning for the word.

Infer must mean "to decide from clues."

Check your Word Wisdom Dictionary to be sure of the meaning.

The word *infer* means "to conclude from thinking carefully about the evidence."

Unlock the Meanings

Practice the Strategy Let's look at another boldfaced word from the article on page 50. Use the context clues strategy on page 51 and follow these steps to figure out the meaning of this word.

instinct

📖 **Read** the sentence that includes the word *instinct* and some of the sentences around it.

🔍 **Look** for context clues to the word's meaning. Do any words describe **What the Word Is Like?**

_____

_____

_____

💡 **Think** about the context clues. What other helpful information do you know?

_____

_____

_____

➡ **Predict** a meaning for the word *instinct*.

_____

_____

_____

✔ **Check** the Word Wisdom Dictionary to be sure of the meaning of *instinct*. Which of the meanings for the word *instinct* fits the context?

_____

_____

_____

✔infer
principle
methodical
conscious
✔instinct
investigate
ingenious
outcome
insight
propose

Use Context Clues   You have been introduced to two vocabulary words from the article about birds' brain power. Those words are checked off in the Word List here. Under "Vocabulary Word" below, write the other eight words from the Word List. Use context clues to predict a meaning for each word under "Your Prediction." Then check the meanings in the Word Wisdom Dictionary. Write the definitions under "Dictionary Says."

Vocabulary Word	Your Prediction	Dictionary Says
1		
2		
3		
4		
5		
6		
7		
8		

Process the Meanings

WORD LIST

- infer
- principle
- methodical
- conscious
- instinct
- investigate
- ingenious
- outcome
- insight
- propose

Choose the Correct Word Write the word from the Word List that belongs in each sentence.

1 To stop the habit of nail biting, you must be

_____ that you are doing it.

2 Jen's careful, _____ approach to problems works.

3 Some fish have a(n) _____ for returning to

a certain place to lay their eggs.

4 I left before the game ended, so I don't know the

_____.

5 By studying ancient ruins, archaeologists gain

_____ into what life was like long ago.

Find the Synonyms Write the word from the Word List that is a synonym for the boldfaced word.

6 "I **suggest** a field trip to an amusement park," offered James.

_____

7 Your plan is **clever**; I wish I'd thought of it. _____

8 Some scientists **study** animal behavior. _____

9 The paw prints and the ripped trash bag led the homeowner to **reason** that a raccoon was in the neighborhood.

_____

10 Repeating an experiment several times is one **rule** of good

science. _____

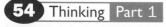

Apply What You've Learned

Relate the Meanings Answer the questions or follow the directions.

1 Give an example of an **instinct** one animal has.

_____

2 Name an activity that requires a **methodical** approach.

_____

3 Name one thing you are **conscious** of each day.

_____

4 Name an important **principle** of American democracy.

_____

5 What was the **outcome** of an exciting game you watched?

_____

6 Name a problem that will be solved with an **ingenious** idea.

_____

7 Why does a good teacher or scientist need good **insight**?

_____

8 What might you **infer** if all the lights in your house went out?

_____

9 How would you **investigate** what made the lights go out?

_____

10 **Propose** a change in a school rule.

_____

Write It! Do you think animals think? Explain your answer. Use several Part 1 vocabulary words.

Latin Roots

for Word Wisdom

Mathematics and Mental Illness:

The Life of John Nash

Despite mental illness, John Nash became one of the twentieth century's greatest mathematicians.

John Nash wanted to discover something new—not a new star or a new species of animal. Nash wanted to discover a new mathematical theory. He wanted to become one of the greatest mathematicians of his time.

In college, Nash focused on different **scientific** fields, like engineering and chemistry. He finally chose to study math. At Princeton University, Nash came up with a new math theory. It was based on the **concept** of game theory. Game theory is the study of making decisions based on probability and statistics.

In 1957 Nash married Alicia Larde. The next year, *Fortune* magazine called Nash one of the world's best mathematicians. He was just thirty years old. This was also the time that he became ill with schizophrenia. This mental illness can cause people to have strange thoughts. They might think people are trying to harm them or that they hear voices. The disease can change their **perception** of the world.

After months of strange behavior, Alicia **supposed** Nash was ill. She put him in a mental hospital. Her **conscience** told her that this was best for him. Over the years, Nash had periods when he was very ill and periods when he was better. Alicia was always there for Nash. So were his friends. They were mathematicians, too. They helped him stay involved with mathematics throughout his illness.

During the 1980s, Nash made some **positive** steps. While it may not have seemed **probable,** John got better little by little. He went back to Princeton for a **purpose**—to again **probe** mathematics. In 1994, John Nash finally received the Nobel Prize in Economics. Thirty years after they had been put to paper, Nash was honored for his ideas about game theory.

Many uninformed people have **preconceived** ideas about mental illness, but these ideas are not the reality. Schizophrenia is a serious mental illness, but John Nash did not let this condition ruin his life. Instead, he went on to become one of the greatest mathematicians of our time.

Practice the Context Clues Strategy Here is one of the boldfaced words from the essay on page 56. Use the context clues strategy you learned in Part 1 on page 51 to figure out the meaning of this word.

scientific

Read the sentence that uses the word *scientific*. Read some of the sentences around the word.

Look for context clues to the word's meaning. Do any words describe **What the Word Is Like?**

_____

_____

_____

Think about the context clues. What other helpful information do you know?

_____

_____

_____

Predict a meaning for the word *scientific*.

_____

_____

_____

Check your Word Wisdom Dictionary to be sure of the meaning of the word *scientific*. Write the definition here.

_____

_____

_____

Unlock the Meanings

Knowing the meaning of some Latin roots will help you decide on the meaning of many English words. All the roots in this part relate to thinking.

Latin Root: **ceiv, cept, cip**
meaning: to take, to seize
English word: *principle*
meaning: a belief or rule

Latin Root: **pos**
meaning: to put, to place
English word: *propose*
meaning: to put forth an idea

Latin Root: **prob, prov**
meaning: to test, to prove
English word: *approve*
meaning: to think well of

Latin Root: **sci**
meaning: to know
English word: *conscious*
meaning: knowing or aware of

Sort by Roots Write each word from the Word List under the correct Latin root below.

WORD LIST

scientific
concept
perception
suppose
conscience
positive
probable
purpose
probe
preconceive

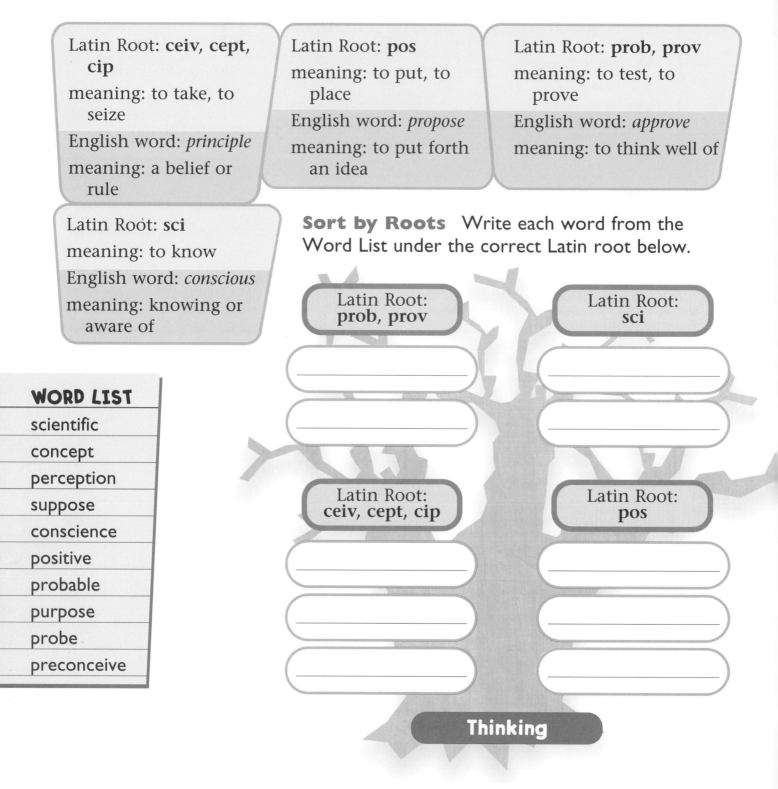

Latin Root: **prob, prov**

Latin Root: **sci**

Latin Root: **ceiv, cept, cip**

Latin Root: **pos**

Thinking

Prefix	Meaning
com-, con-	together
per-	completely
pre-	before

Example

con- (together) + cept (take) = concept

Use Roots and Prefixes Circle the root and any prefix you find in each boldfaced word. Use context clues, roots, and prefixes to write the meaning of each word. Check your definitions in a dictionary.

1 Chris didn't understand the **concept**, so the teacher explained it.

_____

2 Our principal is **probing** the possibility of ordering more computers.

_____

3 If I want to earn money, I **suppose** I can rake leaves for our neighbors.

_____

4 To learn about electricity, Ben Franklin did **scientific** experiments.

_____

5 Since Alliya had not met John, she had no **preconceived** ideas about him.

_____

6 The president's **positive** comments made everyone hopeful.

_____

7 Based on how it acted, our **perception** was that the kitten was scared.

_____

8 She followed her **conscience** and told who took the missing bike.

_____

9 The ball game was cancelled. Bad weather was the **probable** cause.

_____

10 The **purpose** of drama class is to learn how to put on plays.

_____

Process the Meanings

WORD LIST
scientific
concept
perception
suppose
conscience
positive
probable
purpose
probe
preconceive

Identify the Synonyms   Write the best synonym for each boldfaced word.

1 an unusual **concept** _____
    a. problem   b. decision   c. idea

2 **probe** the surface of Mars _____
    a. photograph   b. investigate   c. discover

3 the **probable** cause of the power failure _____
    a. unexpected   b. possible   c. likely

4 **suppose** that you could fly _____
    a. imagine   b. consider   c. dream

5 the main **purpose** for the meeting _____
    a. activity   b. goal   c. rules

Choose the Correct Word   Write the correct word from the Word List to complete each sentence. Underline the parts of the sentence that helped you.

6 Her _____ attitude made us all feel that victory was possible.

7 My _____ that he is taller was corrected when we measured ourselves.

8 Ms. Lee did careful research before writing her _____ book on tornadoes.

9 Ted's _____ helped him know the best way to behave.

10 A _____ opinion is not based on facts.

Apply What You've Learned

Give Reasons Write an answer to each question. Be sure to include the boldfaced words and your reasons in each answer.

1 Is it **probable** that your **conscience** will lead you in the wrong direction?

_____

_____

2 What is your **perception** of people who make **positive** suggestions?

_____

_____

3 How do you **suppose** you would feel if someone had a **preconceived** idea about you?

_____

_____

4 If your teacher were **probing** the class with questions, what might be his or her **purpose**?

_____

_____

5 Would an astronaut use a **scientific** method to better understand the **concept** of gravity?

_____

_____

Speak It! In a small-group discussion, tell about something you have been probing lately. Use as many of the words from the Word List on page 60 as you can.

Reference Skills

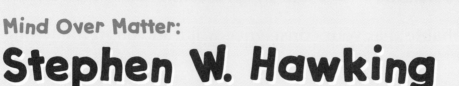

for Word Wisdom

Mind Over Matter:

Stephen W. Hawking

Black holes. Distant galaxies. Time. These are a few of Stephen W. Hawking's favorite subjects. He explored these topics in *A Brief History of Time,* **one of the most popular science books ever written.**

You have heard of Galileo, Isaac Newton, and Albert Einstein. These are some of the greatest scientists of all time. There are others who belong on that list. In fact, one of these scientists is from our lifetime. His name is Stephen W. Hawking.

Stephen Hawking was born in England in 1942. He began college at Oxford when he was seventeen years old. Hawking was **indecisive** about his course of study, but he finally chose to **concentrate** on physics. After a few years, Hawking noticed that he was having physical problems. He was getting clumsy and would fall for no apparent reason. After weeks of hospital tests, Hawking learned he had an incurable disease. The doctors were not sure what it was, but they **concluded** he had only a few years to live. Hawking was only twenty-one years old.

Hawking had a **notion** that he could do something important with his life, even if it was a short one. From then on, he **intended** to study harder than ever. He wanted his life to be meaningful.

Before long, Hawking dove into life and into his research. He began to **formulate** ideas about difficult scientific concepts. He liked to challenge long-accepted theories. Hawking came up with many **logical** ideas about space and time. He liked to **muse** about the beginning of time and life in the universe. Hawking has worked with a group of scientists to try to **compute** what they call "the theory of everything."

Hawking later learned that his disease is ALS, or Lou Gehrig's disease. This disease, over time, destroys the control a person has over his or her muscles. In spite of the odds, Hawking has lived with the disease for decades. He cannot walk, talk, or even move very much. He communicates with a computer that **interprets** his voice from words he chooses on the screen. Hawking is grateful for this invention but says, "The only trouble is that it gives me an American accent."

Practice the Context Clues Strategy Here is one of the boldfaced words from the essay on page 62. Use the context clues strategy you learned in Part 1 on page 51 to figure out the meaning of this word.

concluded

Read the sentence that uses the word *concluded*. Read some of the sentences around the word.

Look for context clues to the word's meaning. Do any words describe **What the Word Is Like?**

_____

_____

_____

Think about the context clues. What other helpful information do you know?

_____

_____

_____

Predict a meaning for the word *conclude*.

_____

_____

_____

Check your Word Wisdom Dictionary to be sure of the meaning of the word *conclude*. Which meaning for *conclude* fits the context?

_____

_____

Looking Up Base Words Most dictionaries do not have a separate main entry for every word in the English language. If a word ends with a common suffix, you will usually have to look up its base word.

If you wanted to find the meaning of the word *preconceived* in a dictionary, you would look up the base word *preconceive*. If you wanted to look up the word *scientifically,* you would find it under the entry for *scientific*.

Find Base Words   Write the base word you would look up in your Word Wisdom Dictionary to find the meaning of each of these words.

1 musing   _____

2 interpreted   _____

3 computes   _____

4 indecisively   _____

5 formulating   _____

6 concentration _____

7 intended   _____

8 logically   _____

9 notions   _____

10 concluding   _____

Find the Meaning

1. Use context clues.
2. Look for a familiar root, prefix, or suffix.
3. If the context or a word part doesn't help, check the dictionary.

Define the Words Use the steps above to write the meaning of each boldfaced word. Write 1, 2, or 3 to show which steps you used.

WORD LIST
indecisive
concentrate
conclude
notion
intend
formulate
logical
muse
compute
interpret

1 I carefully studied my notes before **formulating** a writing plan.

_____

2 The **indecisive** shopper had trouble choosing a new hat.

_____

3 He read about poodles, so he had a **notion** of how they acted.

_____

4 Incomplete research led us to conclusions that weren't **logical**.

_____

5 The loud traffic made it difficult to **concentrate** on homework.

_____

6 I **intend** to practice playing the guitar every day after school.

_____

7 My cousin likes to **muse** about becoming a movie star.

_____

8 Tracks in the snow led us to **conclude** that deer had been here.

_____

9 Dad **computed** the amount of money we need for groceries.

_____

10 Some scientists can **interpret** ancient writing systems.

_____

WORD LIST

- indecisive
- concentrate
- conclude
- notion
- intend
- formulate
- logical
- muse
- compute
- interpret

Complete the Analogies Write a word from the Word List to complete each analogy.

1 Student is to pupil as idea is to _____.

2 Needle is to sew as calculator is to _____.

3 Solve is to problem as _____ is to plan.

4 Art is to creative as science is to _____.

Choose the Correct Meaning For each phrase below, write the word or words that give the best meaning for the boldfaced word.

5 **intended** to become a carpenter _____
      a. planned
      b. asked

6 to **concentrate** on learning French _____
      a. decide to wait
      b. focus attention

7 will **interpret** the poem _____
      a. give a reason for
      b. explain the meaning of

8 an **indecisive** team captain _____
      a. slow in making decisions
      b. not helpful to players

9 **concluded** that the person was guilty _____
      a. wanted to know
      b. came to a decision

10 was **musing** on yesterday's walk _____
      a. thinking deeply
      b. complimenting someone

Apply What You've Learned

Give Examples Write sentences that give an example of each of the following. Use the boldfaced words in your answers.

1 a book you **intend** to read

_____

2 an idea you are **formulating** for a story

_____

3 a time when it is difficult to **concentrate**

_____

4 one thing you are able to **compute**

_____

5 something you have **concluded** about making friends

_____

Complete the Sentences Complete each sentence in a way that shows your understanding of the boldfaced word.

6 Kent's **indecisive** nature made it hard for him to

_____

7 Sonia sat by the pond **musing** about _____

8 Mom's **notion** of proper school dress is _____

9 It is difficult to **interpret** my sister's _____

10 Ms. Sims is a **logical** choice to be our scout leader because

_____

Write It! Describe how you solved a problem you had recently. Use as many words as you can from the Word List on page 66.

Review

for Word Wisdom

WORD LIST

- infer
- principle
- methodical
- conscious
- instinct
- investigate
- ingenious
- outcome
- insight
- propose
- scientific
- concept
- perception
- suppose
- conscience
- positive
- probable
- purpose
- probe
- preconceive
- indecisive
- concentrate
- conclude
- notion
- intend
- formulate
- logical
- muse
- compute
- interpret

Categorize by Prefixes Find words from the Word List that contain the prefixes below. Write the words in the correct group and check them off on the Word List. Write any words you have left in the last column. The number in each heading tells you how many words to list.

Words with the prefix *con-* **or** *com-* ⑥	**Words with the prefix** *in-* **or** *inter-* ⑧	**All Other Words** ⑭

Words with the prefix *per-* **or** *pre-* ②

Use the Clues Write one or more words from the Word List on page 68 for each clue.

1 It is pronounced the same as *principal*. _____

2 Add two letters to *formula*. _____

3 These words have the suffix *-tion*. _____

_____

4 These words have just one syllable. _____

5 Replace the first three letters in *suppose* to get these two words.

_____

Choose the Correct Word Read the sentence and the two words in parentheses. Write the word that makes more sense in the sentence.

6 Scientists ask questions and then _____ the

possible answers. (investigate; preconceive)

7 Add the numbers in a column to _____ the

sum. (compute; interpret)

8 The lawmakers _____ a tax plan.

(inferred; formulated)

9 If you open your mind to others' opinions, your

_____ ideas may change.

(preconceived; scientific)

10 Readers think about what a character says in order to

_____ the character's feelings. (infer; muse)

Taking Vocabulary Tests

Practice Test Fill in the letter of the item that most nearly means the OPPOSITE of the boldfaced word.

1 **concentrated** their efforts
(A) focused
(B) directed
(C) hardened
(D) scattered

2 a surprising **outcome**
(A) income
(B) start
(C) result
(D) ending

3 the most **logical** idea
(A) foolish
(B) lost
(C) sensible
(D) sensitive

4 a **methodical** approach
(A) difficult
(B) slow
(C) careful
(D) unplanned

5 a **positive** comment
(A) negative
(B) clear
(C) hopeful
(D) sure

6 to **conclude** with facts
(A) infer
(B) begin
(C) decide
(D) include

7 her **indecisive** reply
(A) regular
(B) unsure
(C) firm
(D) imaginative

8 **conscious** of his surroundings
(A) frightened
(B) confused
(C) not aware
(D) not tired

9 the **ingenious** plan
(A) satisfying
(B) clever
(C) complex
(D) thoughtless

10 the **probable** result
(A) complete
(B) likely
(C) unlikely
(D) incomplete

Build New Words

Make an Adverb An **adverb** is a word that can describe how something is done. A word can sometimes be turned into an adverb by adding one or two suffixes to it. Add suffixes to these words to form adverbs.

1 positive + ly = _____

2 method + ic + al + ly = _____

3 purpose + ly = _____

4 logic + al + ly = _____

5 ingenious + ly = _____

6 scientific + al + ly = _____

7 concept + ual + ly = _____

8 suppose + ed + ly = _____

9 interpret + ive + ly = _____

10 insight + ful + ly = _____

Speak It! Interview a scientist who studies how animals think, or do a mock interview with a classmate. In your questions, include as many of the words from the Word List on page 68 as you can. Report your findings to the class.

PART 1

Context Clues

for Word Wisdom

A Great Communicator:
Will Rogers

The word *communicate* is related to the word *common*, meaning "shared." Many gifted communicators share their ideas in ways that others understand and enjoy. Will Rogers was a performer whose gift for communicating made him a famous American.

Will Rogers was born in 1879. He was part Cherokee and grew up in Indian territory that later became Oklahoma. Will rode horses and roped cattle, and he loved doing tricks with his lariat, or lasso. He practiced endlessly and competed in roping and riding contests.

As a young man, Will performed in traveling Wild West shows across the country. Later, Will performed in theaters as "The Lariat King." His lasso tricks impressed audiences. He began to add **conversational** remarks about the trick he was about to do. "I don't have any idea that I'll get it, but anyway, here goes," he would **drawl** gently. The audience laughed in appreciation. If he missed a trick, he made another **quip** to get a laugh. Unlike some comedians who **impersonated** various people, Will Rogers seemed real and sincere.

Will's act was more **monologue** than rope tricks. Unlike a rehearsed speech, his comments were **spontaneous**. He used news items to gently **ridicule** the government and joke about current events. "Congress is so strange," he said. "A man gets up to speak and says nothing. Nobody listens; then everybody disagrees."

Unlike some comedians' daring **pronouncements,** Will's were not harsh. Instead, they were truthful, charming, and funny observations. People listened and believed him.

Soon, Will Rogers gained world **acclaim**. He starred on stage, in radio, and in films. He wrote a news column read by millions. He met world leaders. "It's great to be great," he said. "But it's greater to be human." He grew rich, but eagerly gave money to people in need.

When Will Rogers died in a plane crash in 1935, Americans grieved. They lost their cowboy **humorist,** wise observer, and friend.

COMMUNICATION

UNIT 4

Context Clues Strategy

Look for What the Word Is Not Like

EXAMPLE: Unlike the rambling, disorganized talks given by some teachers, Professor Cohen's lectures are *concise*.

CLUE: The sentence tells you that a concise lecture is *"unlike the rambling, disorganized talks."* Therefore it must be organized and purposeful.

Here are the steps for using this context clues strategy to figure out the meaning of the word *impersonate*.

Read the sentence with the unknown word and some of the sentences around it.

*Unlike some comedians who **impersonated** various people, Will Rogers seemed real and sincere.*

Look for context clues. Do any words tell **What the Word Is Not Like**?

The words *unlike some comedians* point out that Will Rogers was different from other comedians who impersonated people. The words *real* and *sincere* show how he was different.

Think about the context clues and other information you may already know.

The word *person* is in *impersonated*.

Predict a meaning for the word.

The word *impersonate* probably means "to pretend to be another person."

Check your Word Wisdom Dictionary to be sure of the meaning.

The word *impersonate* means "to act like or copy the appearance or speech of another person."

🔒 Unlock the Meanings

Practice the Strategy One of the boldfaced words from the article on page 72 appears below. Use the context clues strategy on page 73 to figure out the meaning of this word.

spontaneous

📖 **Read** the sentence that includes the word *spontaneous* and some of the sentences around it.

🔍 **Look** for context clues to the word's meaning. Do any words tell **What the Word Is Not Like**?

_____

_____

_____

💡 **Think** about the context clues. What other helpful information do you know?

_____

_____

_____

➡️ **Predict** a meaning for the word *spontaneous*.

_____

_____

_____

✔️ **Check** your Word Wisdom Dictionary to be sure of the meaning of the word *spontaneous*. Write the dictionary meaning on the line.

_____

_____

Use Context Clues You have been introduced to two vocabulary words from the article about Will Rogers. Those words are checked off in the Word List here. Under "Vocabulary Word," write the other eight words from the Word List. Predict a meaning for each word under "Your Prediction." Then check the meanings in the Word Wisdom Dictionary. Write the definitions under "Dictionary Says."

WORD LIST

conversational

drawl

quip

✔impersonate

monologue

✔spontaneous

ridicule

pronouncement

acclaim

humorist

Vocabulary Word	Your Prediction	Dictionary Says
1		
2		
3		
4		
5		
6		
7		
8		

Process the Meanings

Use the Words Correctly in Writing Rewrite each sentence. Include the word in parentheses in your sentence.

conversational

drawl

quip

impersonate

monologue

spontaneous

ridicule

pronouncement

acclaim

humorist

1 The comedian told jokes for fifteen minutes. (monologue)

_____

2 The unexpected cheers encouraged the football team. (spontaneous)

_____

3 Will Rogers's funny articles and talks made him popular. (humorist)

_____

4 Her slow, drawn-out way of speaking was charming. (drawl)

_____

5 Don't make fun of someone, because your comments may hurt. (ridicule)

_____

6 The speaker used an easy, natural tone. (conversational)

_____

7 It is against the law to pretend to be a police officer. (impersonate)

_____

8 Kay made an important statement. (pronouncement)

_____

9 Jo the clown always had a funny remark ready. (quip)

_____

10 The winning team came home to crowds of fans. (acclaim)

_____

Apply What You've Learned

Relate the Meanings Follow the directions below.

1 Describe a time when you had to act or talk **spontaneously**.

_____

2 What would you do if you were trying to **impersonate** a cat?

_____

3 What have you talked about lately in a **conversational** way?

_____

4 How would you feel if someone **ridiculed** you?

_____

5 In what kinds of movies might actors speak with a **drawl**?

_____

6 How could a spontaneous **quip** help a speaker in a debate?

_____

7 What **pronouncement** does the head jurist make after a trial?

_____

8 What could you do that would likely earn you **acclaim**?

_____

9 When an actor gives a **monologue**, what do the other actors do?

_____

10 Name some people a **humorist** might like to impersonate.

_____

Write It! Write a review of a movie or television show. Use as many vocabulary words from Part 1 as you can.

Latin and Greek Roots

for Word Wisdom

That Doesn't Sound Like English:
Understanding Shakespeare

A lot of people think that the works of William Shakespeare are dull. But Shakespeare entertained his audiences with the same elements that modern movies use: love, suspense, and humor. You just have to understand what you're reading.

Many people **claim** that they get lost when reading a Shakespearean play or when watching one performed. They do not understand the language. They use the **analogy** that Shakespeare's language is a foreign language even though he wrote in English! But there are ways to improve your understanding of Shakespeare's works.

It is helpful to see a Shakespeare play performed live. You can hear the **intonations** in the actors' speech. You can experience the actors performing the **dialogue**. The actors give life to the play's characters and events. For example, a dull character might speak his or her lines in a **monotone** voice. When an exciting event happens, an actor might **exclaim** his or her lines. For example, after King Lear **disclaims** his relation to his daughter in the play *King Lear,* the king of France speaks excitedly about his choice to marry her. This is a very tense moment in the play.

Before you see a play, it's helpful to read a summary of the plot. Many of Shakespeare's plays begin with a **prologue,** or an introduction. But this only summarizes part of the play. If you read a summary, you will understand the main idea of the play. You will know what to expect. Then you can focus on the details.

Another way to get familiar with Shakespeare's language is to watch a play on video. There are a lot of movies based on Shakespeare's plays. Some are set in modern times, and others are set in Shakespeare's time. People have even put Shakespeare's writing to music. Everyone can sing along—from deep, rich **baritones** to high sopranos, and everyone in between!

The more Shakespearean English you hear, the more you will understand it. Maybe someday you can **proclaim** yourself an expert!

Practice the Context Clues Strategy Here is one of the boldfaced words from the essay on page 78. Use the context clues strategy you learned in Part 1 on page 73 to figure out the meaning of this word.

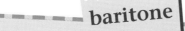
baritone

 Read the sentence that uses the word *baritone*. Read some of the sentences around the word.

🔍 **Look** for context clues to the word's meaning. What clues tell you **What the Word Is Not Like?**

_____

_____

_____

💡 **Think** about the context clues. What other helpful information do you know?

_____

_____

_____

➡ **Predict** a meaning for the word *baritone*.

_____

_____

_____

 Check your Word Wisdom Dictionary to be sure of the meaning of the word *baritone*. Write the definition here.

_____

_____

_____

Unlock the Meanings

You know that some English words have Latin roots. English words can also come from Greek roots. In this unit, you will learn Latin and Greek roots related to communication.

Latin Root: **claim**
meaning: shout, call out
English word: *acclaim*
meaning: public praise

Latin Root: **ton**
meaning: tone
English word: *undertone*
meaning: a low or quiet sound

Greek Root: **log**
meaning: word
English word: *monologue*
meaning: a speech or jokes told by one person

WORD LIST

- claim
- analogy
- intonation
- dialogue
- monotone
- exclaim
- disclaim
- prologue
- baritone
- proclaim

Sort by Roots   Write each word from the Word List under the correct Latin and Greek roots below. Then write other words you know that come from the same Latin and Greek roots.

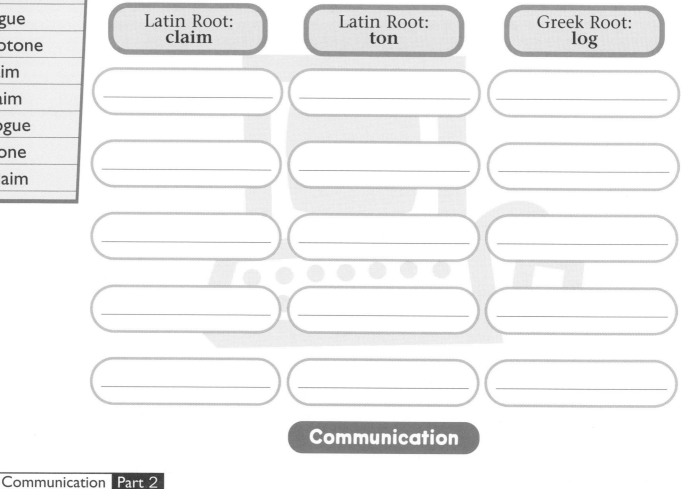

Latin Root: **claim**	Latin Root: **ton**	Greek Root: **log**
_____	_____	_____
_____	_____	_____
_____	_____	_____
_____	_____	_____
_____	_____	_____

Communication

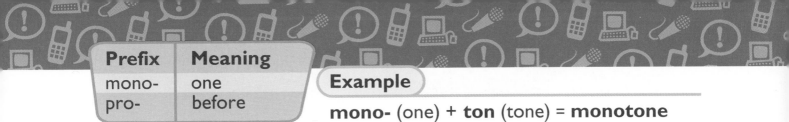

Prefix	Meaning
mono-	one
pro-	before

Example

mono- (one) + **ton** (tone) = **monotone**

Use Roots and Prefixes Circle any root and prefix you find in each boldfaced word. Then use context clues, roots, and prefixes to write the meaning of each word.

1 Unlike a soprano, a **baritone** has a low singing voice.

_____

2 The judge **proclaimed** loudly that Kendal had won the blue ribbon.

_____

3 In act one, two characters in the play have a **dialogue** about camping.

_____

4 The makers of Tasty O's **claim** that their cereal will keep you healthy.

_____

5 Because Yi read the **prologue** first, he knew what the book was about.

_____

6 Voters were bored listening to the candidate speak in a **monotone**.

_____

7 "I can't believe you got me a puppy for my birthday!" she **exclaimed**.

_____

8 Ryan's **analogy** of a spider's web describes our highway system.

_____

9 Leah's **intonation** made her oral report easy to understand.

_____

10 My brother **disclaimed** responsibility for the broken window.

_____

Process the Meanings

WORD LIST

claim

analogy

intonation

dialogue

monotone

exclaim

disclaim

prologue

baritone

proclaim

Complete the Meanings Write the word that best completes the sentence and explains the boldfaced word.

1 A **dialogue** is a(n) _____.
a. speech   b. announcement   c. conversation

2 You use an **analogy** to _____ two things.
a. compare   b. describe   c. explain

3 The singing voice of a **baritone** is _____.
a. high   b. low   c. loud

4 The **prologue** of a play comes at the _____.
a. beginning   b. middle   c. end

5 A **monotone** is a _____ tone of voice.
a. soft   b. harsh   c. single

6 A speaker with good **intonation** changes _____.
a. posture   b. pitch   c. accent

Revise Sentences Rewrite each sentence. Replace the underlined words with a word from the Word List. You may have to add an ending.

7 "I can't believe I won!" he said <u>loudly with surprise</u>.

_____

8 My voice teacher <u>states as a fact</u> that she can teach anyone to sing.

_____

9 The students <u>said they didn't have</u> any knowledge of the classroom prank.

_____

10 The newly elected mayor will <u>officially announce</u> victory tomorrow evening.

_____

Apply What You've Learned

Give Reasons Answer each question with **yes** or **no**. Give reasons for your answers.

1 Could a robbery suspect **disclaim** responsibility?

_____

2 Could a suspect **proclaim** his or her innocence of a crime?

_____

3 Are you likely to read a **prologue** in the newspaper?

_____

4 Is the **dialogue** of a play usually written in the program?

_____

5 Could someone **claim** that they had been to Japan?

_____

6 Do you expect actors in a movie to speak in a **monotone**?

_____

Name the Categories Write a word from the Word List to complete each list below. Then tell what category all the words belong to.

	Word	Category
7 alto, tenor,	_____	_____
8 simile, metaphor,	_____	_____
9 shout, holler,	_____	_____
10 volume, rate,	_____	_____

Speak It! Create an announcement for a real or imaginary play. Deliver your announcement to your class. Use some words from the Part 2 Word List.

PART 3 Reference Skills

The Internet:

See History Come to Life

How do you like to learn about history? You can read books, visit museums, or watch movies. But did you know that you can also learn about history on the Internet?

Maybe you think history is boring. Who cares what happened long ago? You might think history is just words and photographs in a book. Well, there's a place where history comes to life. On the Internet you can hear and see history.

There are Web sites that have recorded history. Some college teachers have recordings of their **lectures** online. You can also find famous speeches on the Internet. You can listen to Martin Luther King Jr. **assert** his belief in equal rights. You can hear Albert Einstein **declare** that the use of atomic bombs is a terrible thing. You can hear Thomas Edison **elaborate** on his discoveries in electricity. You actually hear these important people from history!

And history does not just mean politics and science; it also means culture. You can listen to singers John Lennon and Paul McCartney offer an **expression** of the importance of music. You'll hear Babe Ruth **insist** that baseball is the best game in the world. There are some recordings that sound unclear. This might be because the **acoustics** in the recording location were not very good. But overall, you get a feel for the historical moment.

If audio is not enough for you, you can watch video clips, too. You might watch a news clip where experts **converse** about a certain topic. Do you want to watch American astronauts put the flag on the moon? Visit the NASA Web site. In fact, you can find clips from many historical events. All you have to do is search. The Internet does not hide history away; it **accentuates** how interesting history can be.

Written documents are also important to history. At the Web site of the U.S. National Archives, you can see many important documents in our country's history. There are even copies of famous **petitions** online—you can actually view the signatures of the people who signed them!

New things are added to the Internet every day. Take a look and see what you can find. You'll see that history is very exciting!

Practice the Context Clues Strategy Here is one of the boldfaced words from the essay on page 84. Use the context clues strategy you learned in Part 1 on page 73 to figure out the meaning of this word.

accentuates

Read the sentence that uses the word *accentuates*. Read some of the sentences around the word.

Look for context clues to the word's meaning. Do any words tell **What the Word Is Not Like**?

_____

_____

_____

Think about the context clues. What other helpful information do you know?

_____

_____

_____

Predict a meaning for the word *accentuate*.

_____

_____

_____

 Check your Word Wisdom Dictionary to be sure of the meaning of the word *accentuate*. Write the definition here.

_____

_____

_____

Multiple Meanings Because many English words have more than one meaning, you will often find more than one definition in a dictionary entry. Each definition is numbered. Read the five different meanings for the word *expression*.

expression[1] /ik **spresh'** ən/ *n.* the act of communicating, as in words. *Pam's speech was an expression of her ideas.*

expression[2] /ik **spresh'** ən/ *n.* something that communicates an opinion or a feeling. *The flowers were an expression of our sorrow.*

expression[3] /ik **spresh'** ən/ *n.* a look on one's face that shows feelings. *Jordan's serious expression meant things were going badly.*

expression[4] /ik **spresh'** ən/ *n.* a way of speaking, singing, or playing that shows a certain feeling. *Our teacher read the poem with great expression.*

expression[5] /ik **spresh'** ən/ *n.* a particular word or phrase. *I hear the common expression "Exercise your right to vote!" around election day.*

Choose Definitions Using the dictionary entries above, write 1, 2, 3, 4, or 5 to tell which meaning of *expression* is used in the sentence.

1 ____ Carmen played her piano solo with great **expression**.

2 ____ The essay contained an **expression** of his thoughts.

3 ____ All the children at the beach had joyful **expressions**.

4 ____ Mom uses the **expression** "spick and span."

5 ____ Tears can sometimes be an **expression** of happiness.

Find the Meaning

1. Use context clues.
2. Look for a familiar root, prefix, or suffix.
3. If the context or a word part doesn't help, check the dictionary.

Define the Words Follow the steps above to decide on the meaning of each boldfaced word. Write the meaning of the word. Then write 1, 2, or 3 to show which steps you used.

WORD LIST

lecture
assert
declare
elaborate
expression
insist
acoustics
converse
accentuate
petition

1 They signed a **petition** asking the city for a recycling program.

_____

2 The great **acoustics** in the concert hall allowed us to hear well.

_____

3 He **asserted** that more tax money should be spent on education.

_____

4 Her handmade gift for me was an **expression** of friendship.

_____

5 Dad **insisted** that we finish our work before going to the park.

_____

6 The speaker gave her **lecture** on comets from a museum stage.

_____

7 My best friend and I **converse** on the phone almost every day.

_____

8 Your bright blue shirt **accentuates** the color of your eyes.

_____

9 Please **elaborate** on your report by adding more examples.

_____

10 The principal **declared** that skates are not allowed in school.

_____

Process the Meanings

WORD LIST

lecture

assert

declare

elaborate

expression

insist

acoustics

converse

accentuate

petition

Identify the Synonyms Write the word that is the best synonym for each boldfaced word.

1 **accentuate** his good qualities _____

    a. find   b. stress   c. notice

2 to **converse** for hours _____

    a. talk   b. rest   c. travel

3 to **insist** that we all wear hats _____

    a. ask   b. agree   c. demand

4 **elaborated** on her idea _____

    a. decided   b. concentrated   c. expanded

5 a **lecture** about Abraham Lincoln _____

    a. book   b. speech   c. discussion

6 **asserted** that his team would win _____

    a. claimed   b. hoped   c. planned

Choose the Correct Word Write the correct word from the Word List to complete each sentence. You may need to add an ending. Underline any parts of the sentence that helped you make your choice.

7 Kris collected voters' signatures on a _____.

8 The food basket was an _____ of thanks.

9 Ben loudly _____ that we should cook dinner.

10 Improved _____ in the theater helped

audiences hear the performance better.

Apply What You've Learned

Demonstrate Word Knowledge Use what you have learned about the boldfaced words to answer each question.

1 During a water shortage, what is a governor likely to **declare**?

_____

2 What might two doctors **converse** about?

_____

3 How could a speaker begin a **lecture**?

_____

4 What might a confident student **assert**?

_____

Complete the Sentences Complete each sentence in a way that shows your understanding of the boldfaced word.

5 The artist **accentuated** the painting by _____

6 Voters signed a **petition** asking _____

7 As an **expression** of her gratitude, she _____

8 The room's **acoustics** were so poor that _____

_____

9 She **elaborated** on her story by _____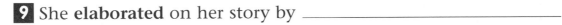

10 I didn't play well, so the coach **insisted** _____

_____

Write It! Write a speech on a topic you know well. Use words from the Word List on page 88.

Review

for Word Wisdom

What's the Root? Choose words from the Word List to write in each section below. The number in each heading tells you how many words to list. Some words will be listed twice.

WORD LIST

- conversational
- drawl
- quip
- impersonate
- monologue
- spontaneous
- ridicule
- pronouncement
- acclaim
- humorist
- claim
- analogy
- intonation
- dialogue
- monotone
- exclaim
- disclaim
- prologue
- baritone
- proclaim
- lecture
- assert
- declare
- elaborate
- expression
- insist
- acoustics
- converse
- accentuate
- petition

Words with the Latin root *claim* meaning "shout" 5

Words with the Greek root *log* meaning "word" 4

Words with the Latin root *ton* meaning "tone" 3

Verbs that can mean "to say strongly or firmly" 8

Choose One of Two Read the sentence and the two words in parentheses. Circle the word that makes more sense in the sentence.

1 Nobody planned it, but the whole audience joined the performer in a ___ sing-along. (converse   spontaneous)

2 Musicians prefer to play in rooms that have good ___. (acoustics   lectures)

3 Many voters signed the ___ for improving the town parks. (pronouncement   petition)

4 This gift is a small ___ of our thanks. (quip   expression)

5 It is useful to ___ often when learning a new language. (converse   impersonate)

Answer True or False Read each statement. If the statement is True, circle **T**. If the statement is False, circle **F**. Then give a reason for your choice.

6 Fast-talking people tend to **drawl**.   T   F

_____

7 Writers add details to **elaborate** on their ideas.   T   F

_____

8 When you make a **quip**, you hope people will laugh.   T   F

_____

9 Recycling is a **conversational** activity.   T   F

_____

10 It is possible to **impersonate** someone when talking.   T   F

_____

Taking Vocabulary Tests

Some multiple-choice tests ask you to choose a word that fits in a sentence. Start by reading the sentence to yourself, saying "blank" for the missing word. Think about a meaning that seems to make sense in the blank. Then try each of the answer choices. Choose the one that matches the meaning you thought about.

Sample:

Fill in the letter of the answer that BEST fits in the sentence.

The hungry baby woke up ____ from her nap.

(A) sleeping
(B) crying
(C) smiling
(D) giggling

Practice Test   Fill in the letter of the answer that BEST fits in the sentence.

1 The worker unwisely ____ his boss.
(A) ridiculed
(B) proclaimed
(C) declared
(D) quipped

2 The ____ sang beautifully.
(A) monotone
(B) baritone
(C) expression
(D) analogy

3 The judge's ____ was harsh.
(A) quip
(B) pronouncement
(C) prologue
(D) monotone

4 The ____ writes amusing stories.
(A) baritone
(B) petition
(C) dialogue
(D) humorist

5 An actor ____ President Abraham Lincoln.
(A) impersonated
(B) conversed
(C) proclaimed
(D) elaborated

6 The topic of the ____ was "Saving Money."
(A) intonation
(B) acclaim
(C) lecture
(D) acoustics

7 The actor's ____ was funny.
(A) spontaneous
(B) lecture
(C) dialogue
(D) humorist

8 I fell asleep listening to the ____ voice of the speaker.
(A) conversing
(B) exclaiming
(C) conversational
(D) monotone

9 The speaker ____ her point by pounding on the table.
(A) accentuated
(B) drawled
(C) disclaimed
(D) petitioned

10 Give examples to ____ on your idea.
(A) impersonate
(B) converse
(C) elaborate
(D) declare

Play with Language

Find the Hidden Message Choose the word from the box that matches each clue. Write the letters of that word in the boxes.

| humorist | converse | proclaim | analogy | acclaim |
| prologue | monologue | lecture | petition | acoustics |

Clues

1 This comes before a story.

2 A comedian performs this.

3 Voters sign this.

4 This is one kind of entertainer.

5 An expert's talk is often called this.

6 This means "to discuss."

7 This means "to announce."

8 This is a kind of comparison.

9 This is the study of sound.

10 This is what fame seekers want.

What does a great communicator need? To answer that question, write the letters from the shaded boxes in order:

_____

Speak It! Give some advice to help others improve their speaking ability. Use as many words as you can from the Word List on page 90.

Context Clues

for Word Wisdom

Land of Ice:

Antarctica

Find a globe, and point to your city or town. Then move your finger south until it reaches the bottom of the globe. Your finger is on Antarctica, Earth's southern-most continent. Read this informational article to learn about Antarctica.

Imaginary lines of **longitude** run north and south over the surface of the earth. They are used to locate places on our planet. The lines meet on the dome of each **hemisphere** at the North Pole and the South Pole. The land that surrounds the South Pole is Antarctica, the fifth largest continent on Earth.

Antarctica is a **unique** land of extremes. It is the coldest place on Earth. The winter temperature has been measured at a record-breaking -89° Celsius (-128° Fahrenheit). Summer temperatures rarely rise above freezing. It is the windiest place on Earth, too. Bitter winds blast coastal areas at 190 kilometers (118 miles) per hour. Antarctica is also one of the driest lands on Earth. Inland, it receives only about 5 centimeters (2 inches) of snowfall a year. Because of the **frigid** temperatures, very little of the snow melts. This results in **massive** layers of ice covering almost all of Antarctica. The

average thickness of the ice is more than 2 kilometers (about 1¼ miles)!

Few plants and animals live on this icy land. In contrast, life is abundant in the surrounding ocean. Vast quantities of tiny **microscopic** plants and animals drift in the water. They are the basic food supply for fish, birds, seals, and whales.

The people who know Antarctica best are scientists. At research **sites**, scientists gather all sorts of information. They study wildlife, rocks, the ocean, sunlight, and the atmosphere. Some scientists study ice. They use drilling **devices** to lift out layers of ice. The layers hold clues about Earth's climate over many thousands of years. Scientists look at past **variations** to predict future climate changes.

Antarctica is hard to reach, a **solitary** continent far from home. For curious scientists, however, Antarctica is one of the best places to learn about Earth.

Context Clues Strategy

Look for What the Word Is Used For

EXAMPLE: The best-known birds of Antarctica are penguins, whose *adaptations* allow them to survive the harsh winters.

CLUE: The phrase *to survive the harsh winters* tells what *adaptations* are used for.

Here are the steps for using this context clues strategy to figure out the meaning of the word *longitude*.

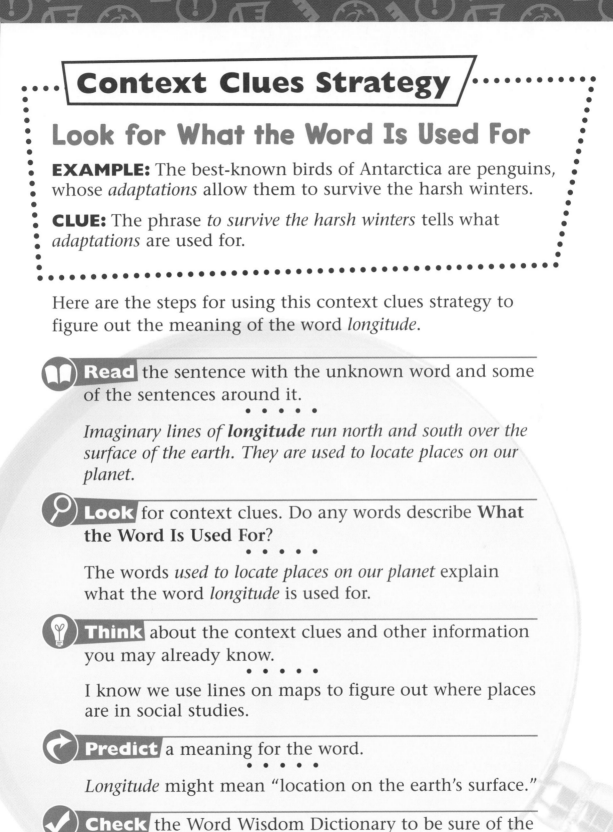

Read the sentence with the unknown word and some of the sentences around it.

• • • • •

*Imaginary lines of **longitude** run north and south over the surface of the earth. They are used to locate places on our planet.*

Look for context clues. Do any words describe **What the Word Is Used For?**

• • • • •

The words *used to locate places on our planet* explain what the word *longitude* is used for.

Think about the context clues and other information you may already know.

• • • • •

I know we use lines on maps to figure out where places are in social studies.

Predict a meaning for the word.

• • • • •

Longitude might mean "location on the earth's surface."

Check the Word Wisdom Dictionary to be sure of the meaning.

• • • • •

The word *longitude* means "distance on the earth's surface, measured east or west from the prime meridian."

Unlock the Meanings

Practice the Strategy A boldfaced word from the article on page 94 is in the box below. Use the context clues strategy on page 95 to figure out the meaning of this word.

devices

Read the sentence that includes the word *devices* and some of the sentences around it.

Look for context clues to the word's meaning. Do any words describe **What the Word Is Used For?**

_____

_____

_____

Think about the context clues. What other helpful information do you know?

_____

_____

_____

Predict a meaning for the word *device*.

_____

_____

_____

Check your Word Wisdom Dictionary to be sure of the meaning of *device*. Write the meaning here.

_____

_____

Use Context Clues   Two words you have learned from the article are checked off in the Word List. In the first column, write the other eight words from the Word List. In the second column, predict a meaning for each word. Look up the meaning in your Word Wisdom Dictionary. Write the dictionary meaning in the third column.

WORD LIST

✔longitude

hemisphere

unique

frigid

massive

microscopic

site

✔device

variation

solitary

	Vocabulary Word	Your Prediction	Dictionary Says
1			
2			
3			
4			
5			
6			
7			
8			

Process the Meanings

WORD LIST

longitude

hemisphere

unique

frigid

massive

microscopic

site

device

variation

solitary

Find Synonyms Write the word from the Word List that is a synonym for the boldfaced word or words in each sentence below.

1 Antarctica is in the southern **half of the earth**.

_____

2 A **lone** ship sailed into the sea of ice.

_____

3 **Extremely small** life forms survive inside rocks.

_____

4 Some icebergs are as **huge** as islands.

_____

5 The weather scientist used a balloon as a measuring **tool**.

_____

6 The South Pole is a **place** for scientific research.

_____

7 Antarctica is a **one-of-a-kind** continent.

_____

8 Antarctic winters are dark and **extremely cold**.

_____

9 One **difference** among the species of penguins is size.

_____

10 Sailors keep track of their ship's **east-west position**.

_____

Apply What You've Learned

Explain Differences Write the answer to each question.

1 What is the difference between a **sphere** and a **hemisphere**?

_____

2 Would you want a **unique** haircut or an **ordinary** one? Why?

_____

3 Would you prefer to be outdoors on a **chilly** day or a **frigid** day?

Why? _____

4 What is the difference between a **massive** desk and a **messy**

desk? _____

5 How is a **site** different from a **sight**?

_____

Tell Why Read each statement. Tell why the statement is true.

6 New York City and San Francisco are at different **longitudes**.

_____

7 Reading can be a **solitary** activity.

_____

8 Germs that cause illness are **microscopic**.

_____

9 A thermometer is a **device** for measuring temperature.

_____

10 Some places have extreme **variations** in temperature.

_____

Write It! Write a paragraph for a tourist brochure advertising Antarctica. Use as many words from Part 1 as you can.

Latin Roots

for Word Wisdom

Singing Together:

Merry Measures

Choral singing is everywhere. There are church choirs. There are school choirs. And there are professional choruses in cities around the world. But what is choral singing really all about?

If you like **solitude,** then choral singing is not for you. Working with others is one of the most important parts of choral singing. Think of it as a team sport: Everyone must work together in order to do well. It is this "working together" that gives a chorus its sense of **unity**. It is not individual singers; it is many singers forming one thing.

In a chorus the singers often sing in **unison,** blending their voices together. But it is not always everyone singing at once. Sometimes, **various** parts of the chorus will take turns singing. These different groups within the larger chorus might be separated by singing style. One group might have high singing voices. Another group might have low singing voices. These groups might even take turns singing different lines of a song. These kinds of changes add **variety** to the style and sound of a chorus.

There are other moments of variety in choral singing. Sometimes, one singer will sing a part of a song alone. In a performance, this **soloist** may or may not stand apart from the rest of the chorus. Some choruses will sing along with an orchestra that provides instrumental music to the program. These choruses are often called symphony choruses. Other choruses are the **sole** music-makers on stage. They make music with their voices alone.

Choruses come in all sizes; the sizes are **variable**. A small town's chorus might have fewer than twenty members. A chorus in a major city might have a few hundred people. All chorus members must have an understanding of music. They must know the **units** for measuring music. They must know how each musical key sounds. Choruses may be different all around the world, but these details of music are **universal** for all.

If you love music, treat yourself to seeing a choral performance. You will be amazed at how skillful the singers are at blending their voices. And you might learn something about working together!

Practice the Context Clues Strategy   Here is one of the boldfaced words from the essay on page 100. Use the context clues strategy you learned in Part 1 on page 95 to figure out the meaning of this word.

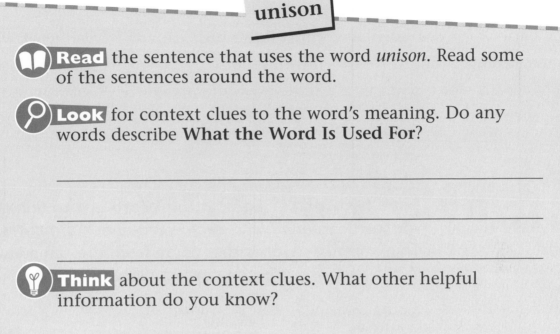

unison

Read the sentence that uses the word *unison*. Read some of the sentences around the word.

Look for context clues to the word's meaning. Do any words describe **What the Word Is Used For**?

_____

_____

_____

Think about the context clues. What other helpful information do you know?

_____

_____

_____

Predict a meaning for the word *unison*.

_____

_____

_____

Check your Word Wisdom Dictionary to be sure of the meaning of the word *unison*. Write the definition here.

_____

_____

_____

🔑 Unlock the Meanings

The Latin roots that you will learn in this unit are all related to measurement. See if you can tell how all the words with the same root are related in meaning.

Latin Root: **sol, soli**
meaning: alone
English word: *solitary*
meaning: being alone

Latin Root: **uni**
meaning: one
English word: *unique*
meaning: one of a kind

Latin Root: **vari**
meaning: many
English word: *variation*
meaning: a slightly different kind

WORD LIST

- solitude
- unity
- unison
- various
- variety
- soloist
- sole
- variable
- unit
- universal

Sort by Roots Look at the Word List to find the roots that you just learned. Write each word under the correct root. Think of other words that come from the same Latin root. Write each word in the correct place.

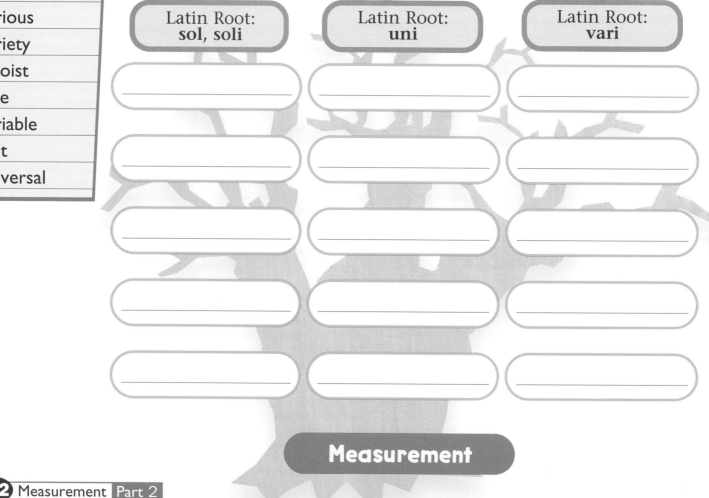

Latin Root: **sol, soli**

Latin Root: **uni**

Latin Root: **vari**

Measurement

Use Roots Circle the root in each boldfaced word. Then use your knowledge of roots and context clues to write the meaning of each word. Check your definitions in the Word Wisdom Dictionary.

1 We planted a **variety** of flowers, including mums, roses, and pansies.

_____

2 Aram's **sole** reason for taking the trip was to see the Grand Canyon.

_____

3 All people understand the **universal** need for food and shelter.

_____

4 Standing in front of the orchestra, the **soloist** played her violin.

_____

5 A meter is a **unit** of length used to measure distances.

_____

6 The size of the crowd at our soccer matches is **variable**.

_____

7 Our whole class answered the question in **unison**.

_____

8 To find **solitude**, I leave the city and go to the desert.

_____

9 We looked at **various** computers and bought the silver laptop.

_____

10 The countries showed **unity** by signing a trade agreement.

_____

WORD LIST

solitude
unity
unison
various
variety
soloist
sole
variable
unit
universal

Match the Synonyms   Match each vocabulary word with its synonym. Write the synonym on the line.

Vocabulary Word	Synonym
1 universal _____	oneness
2 variable _____	assortment
3 sole _____	global
4 variety _____	only
5 unity _____	changeable

Complete the Meanings   Write the word that best completes each sentence.

6 Someone who enjoys **solitude** likes being

_____.

    a. alone   b. outdoors   c. inside

7 When people sing in **unison**, they sing

_____.

    a. quietly   b. one at a time   c. together

8 A **soloist** usually performs _____ by himself or herself.
    a. comedy   b. gymnastics   c. music

9 If people are reading **various** books, the books are all

_____.

    a. interesting   b. different   c. difficult

10 A **unit** is an exact _____ used for measuring.
    a. amount   b. weight   c. scale

Apply What You've Learned

Find Examples Read each description below. Then put a **check mark (✓)** beside every example that matches the description.

1 what you're likely to see a **soloist** do

_____ sing a song   _____ play a trumpet

_____ announce an act   _____ do a trick

2 places you could find **solitude**

_____ in your room   _____ in a crowded mall

_____ on a mountaintop   _____ at a basketball game

3 **units** of measurement

_____ gram   _____ ruler

_____ hour   _____ pint

4 things that are **variable**

_____ the weather   _____ a person's mood

_____ students in school   _____ days in a week

5 acting in **unison**

_____ teachers in a dialogue   _____ classmates reciting a poem

_____ brothers playing catch   _____ dancers doing steps

Find Correct Uses Decide whether the boldfaced word has been used correctly. Write **C** for **correct** or **I** for **incorrect**.

6 The team showed **unity** by cheering for all the players. _____

7 Every Friday we rent **various** movies at the video store. _____

8 Earth is the **sole** planet among all the planets. _____

9 Humans have a **universal** need for water. _____

10 Because of the **variety** in temperature, I wore a jacket. _____

Speak It! Give a short talk describing your favorite kind of music and tell why it is your favorite. Use as many of the words from Part 2 as possible.

PART 3

Reference Skills

for Word Wisdom

Food Science:

Measuring Cookies

Have you ever thought about cookies? Of course you have. But have you ever *really* thought about cookies? Read this article to learn more about the science of baking.

When you think about science, you might picture a scientist in a white lab coat. She is pouring a steaming liquid into a beaker. But there is more to science. It is all around us, even in the kitchen.

A cookie recipe is a scientific, **enumerated** list of food ingredients. Bakers **calculate** the proper mixture of ingredients by experimenting just like scientists do. That's why a baker is sometimes called a food scientist.

To find the perfect recipe, a baker will try many versions of the same recipe. He will **evaluate** how changes in the recipe affect the final product. The baker will keep track of these differences. When the experiment is finished, a **comparison** of the results identifies the tastiest cookie!

Each of the basic cookie ingredients has a job. To get the best cookies, you must use **accurate** amounts of the ingredients. Baking is a precise science. In regular cooking, you can **estimate** how much of something you need to use. In baking, guessing about amounts is not a good idea. Science might decide to ruin your recipe for you!

Most cookie recipes begin with flour. Some kinds of flour make cookies soft, while others make cookies crunchy. A recipe will **identify** which kind of flour is best. Cookies also use sugar. Sugar is not just for taste. The chemical properties in sugar help make a cookie's shape. Certain kinds of sugar will make cookies thin and wide. Other kinds **reduce** a cookie's ability to spread out, making them thick and compact.

Without a leavening agent, cookies would be as hard and flat as crackers! Baking powder is a good leavening agent. When you add a liquid to baking powder, carbon dioxide **accumulates**. Carbon dioxide produces bubbles like the bubbles in soda. In cookies, these bubbles help **inflate** the dough, making it fluffy.

Of course, chocolate chips, oatmeal, raisins, and nuts all give cookies flavor. Ask an adult to help you experiment with cookie recipes. Maybe you will want to be a food scientist someday!

Practice the Context Clues Strategy Here is one of the boldfaced words from the article on page 106. Use the context clues strategy you learned in Part 1 on page 95 to figure out the meaning of this word.

inflate

Read the sentence that uses the word *inflate*. Read some of the sentences around the word.

Look for context clues to the word's meaning. Do any words describe **What the Word Is Used For?**

_____

_____

_____

Think about the context clues. What other helpful information do you know?

_____

_____

_____

Predict a meaning for the word *inflate*.

_____

_____

_____

Check your Word Wisdom Dictionary to be sure of the meaning of the word *inflate*. Which of the meanings for *inflate* fits the context? Write the definition here.

_____

_____

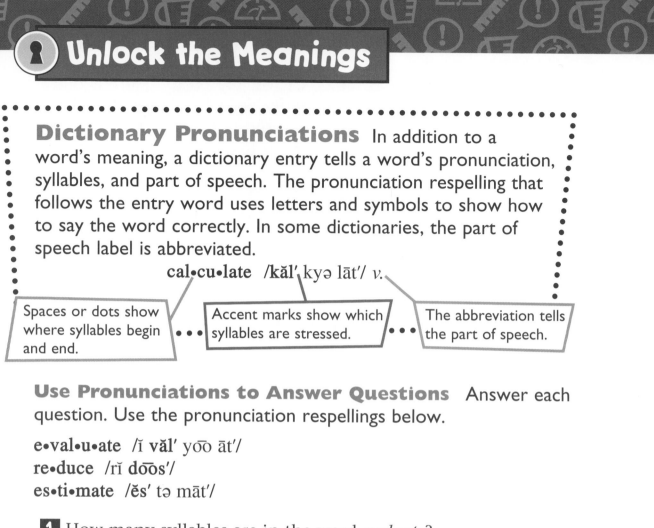

Dictionary Pronunciations In addition to a word's meaning, a dictionary entry tells a word's pronunciation, syllables, and part of speech. The pronunciation respelling that follows the entry word uses letters and symbols to show how to say the word correctly. In some dictionaries, the part of speech label is abbreviated.

cal•cu•late /kăl′ kyə lāt′/ *v.*

Spaces or dots show where syllables begin and end.

Accent marks show which syllables are stressed.

The abbreviation tells the part of speech.

Use Pronunciations to Answer Questions Answer each question. Use the pronunciation respellings below.

e•val•u•ate /ĭ văl′ yo͞o āt′/
re•duce /rĭ do͞os′/
es•ti•mate /ĕs′ tə māt′/

1 How many syllables are in the word *evaluate*? _____

2 Which syllable in *reduce* is stressed? _____

3 Which syllables in *evaluate* are stressed? _____

4 Which syllable in *reduce* has a short vowel sound? _____

5 Which syllable in *estimate* has a long vowel sound? _____

6 How many syllables are in *reduce*? _____

7 How many syllables are in *estimate*? _____

8 Which syllables in *estimate* are stressed? _____

9 Which syllables in *evaluate* have a long vowel sound? _____

10 Which syllables in *estimate* have a short vowel sound? _____

! **Find the Meaning**

1. Use context clues.
2. Look for a familiar root, prefix, or suffix.
3. If the context or a word part doesn't help, check the dictionary.

Define the Words Follow the steps above to write the meaning of each boldfaced word. Then write 1, 2, or 3 to show which steps you used.

WORD LIST

enumerate
calculate
evaluate
comparison
accurate
estimate
identify
reduce
accumulate
inflate

1 Adam was able to **reduce** his weight with exercise.

_____

2 You can use a hand pump to **inflate** bicycle tires.

_____

3 The pilot **estimated** the flight would take five hours, but she wasn't sure.

_____

4 My **comparison** of the two movies showed their similarities.

_____

5 She carefully checked her report to be sure that it was **accurate**.

_____

6 Jason hopes to **accumulate** many fossils for his collection.

_____

7 The lifeguard **enumerated** the safety rules for using the pool.

_____

8 To **identify** some kinds of birds, Luis listens to their songs.

_____

9 Knowing the speed of light helped Lindsay **calculate** the distance to the star.

_____

10 Our teacher gave us a checklist to **evaluate** our essays.

_____

Process the Meanings

WORD LIST

enumerate

calculate

evaluate

comparison

accurate

estimate

identify

reduce

accumulate

inflate

Identify Synonyms Write the word that is the best synonym for each boldfaced word.

1 an **accurate** measurement _____
   a. identical   b. excellent   c. exact

2 to **reduce** the amount _____
   a. guess   b. decrease   c. measure

3 **enumerated** their reasons _____
   a. spelled   b. listed   c. added

4 quietly **accumulating** nuts for winter

_____

   a. growing   b. hiding   c. gathering

5 could **identify** the suspect _____
   a. recognize   b. locate   c. help

6 **evaluated** each skater's performance

_____

   a. judged   b. enjoyed   c. watched

Revise Sentences Rewrite each sentence. Replace the underlined words with a vocabulary word. You may have to add an ending to the word.

7 Aunt Kate <u>used math to figure out</u> the cost of a vacation.

_____

8 We <u>figured out roughly</u> the number of cars on the road.

_____

9 Our <u>study of similarities</u> in cameras led us to buy this one.

_____

10 The raft must be <u>expanded with air</u> before you can use it.

_____

Apply What You've Learned

Give Examples   Write a sentence that gives an example for each description below. Use the boldfaced words in your answers.

1 a country you can **identify** on a map or a globe

_____

2 something you are **accumulating** in your locker or room

_____

3 a way you can **evaluate** your progress in school

_____

4 a time when it is important for you to be **accurate**

_____

5 something in nature that can't be **calculated**

_____

6 a point of **comparison** between two dogs

_____

7 something that can be **inflated**

_____

8 something that should be **reduced**

_____

9 something that you have to **estimate**

_____

10 one right that is **enumerated** in the Constitution

_____

Write It!   Write questions you would ask a scientist in an interview. Use as many of the words from Part 3 as you can.

Review

for Word Wisdom

Sort by Categories Write the words from the Word List that belong in each section below. The number in each heading tells you how many words to list.

WORD LIST

longitude
hemisphere
unique
frigid
massive
microscopic
site
device
variation
solitary
solitude
unity
unison
various
variety
soloist
sole
variable
unit
universal
enumerate
calculate
evaluate
comparison
accurate
estimate
identify
reduce
accumulate
inflate

Words having to do with likenesses or differences (5)

Words that begin with a Latin root meaning "one" (5)

Adjectives that describe size (2)

Verbs that mean "to count or measure" (3)

Choose the Correct Words Write the word from the Word List on page 112 that completes each sentence.

1 We cheered after the _____ sang.

2 The United States is in Earth's western _____.

3 The store will _____ the price of shoes.

4 You can _____ if you don't know the exact amount.

5 Open the freezer to feel the _____ air.

6 A pump is a _____ for moving water from one place to another.

7 James enjoys being with crowds, but Jamal prefers _____.

8 Bacteria are _____ creatures.

9 The pound is one _____ of measurement.

10 People speak different languages, but a smile has _____ meaning.

Recognize Correct Sentences Write **yes** or **no** to tell whether each sentence uses the boldfaced word correctly.

11 _____ The **longitude** of my trip was too long.

12 _____ The restaurant offers **various** pasta dishes.

13 _____ **Calculate** your math problems before you leave.

14 _____ I should **accumulate** to get rid of this stuff.

15 _____ She lost her **site** and couldn't read.

Taking Vocabulary Tests

Some vocabulary tests ask you to complete analogies. The test gives you one pair of words that are related. The test then gives you a third word; for example: Shoe is to foot as hat is to_____. You choose the word that completes the statement. A good strategy is to think about the relationship of the words. Relationships include synonyms, antonyms, and what things are used for. Make a statement with the first pair of words and see which word makes the same statement for the next pair.

Sample:

Fill in the letter by the answer that BEST completes the analogy.
Warm is to hot as **cool** is to_____.

ⓐ bubbles
ⓑ wet
ⓒ air
ⓓ cold

Practice Test Fill in the letter by the answer that BEST completes the analogy.

1 Break is to build as **reduce** is to _____.
Ⓐ increase
Ⓑ broken
Ⓒ lower
Ⓓ weight

2 Hands are to clock as **longitude** is to _____.
Ⓐ hour
Ⓑ globe
Ⓒ measurement
Ⓓ circle

3 Path is to walkway as **site** is to _____.
Ⓐ seeing
Ⓑ street
Ⓒ footstep
Ⓓ setting

4 Instruct is to lesson as **evaluate** is to _____.
Ⓐ learning
Ⓑ athlete
Ⓒ student
Ⓓ test

5 One is to many as **sole** is to _____.
Ⓐ nobody
Ⓑ alone
Ⓒ numerous
Ⓓ shoe

6 Lose is to fail as **accumulate** is to _____.
Ⓐ excel
Ⓑ gather
Ⓒ miss
Ⓓ game

7 Name is to label as **identify** is to _____.
Ⓐ misspell
Ⓑ count
Ⓒ recognize
Ⓓ person

8 Breathe is to lungs as **inflate** is to_____.
Ⓐ balloon
Ⓑ mind
Ⓒ collapse
Ⓓ heart

9 Honest is to truthful as **accurate** is to _____.
Ⓐ false
Ⓑ correct
Ⓒ familiar
Ⓓ secret

10 Abundant is to many as **solitary** is to _____.
Ⓐ variety
Ⓑ massive
Ⓒ unity
Ⓓ one

Build New Words

Use the Noun Suffixes *-ion*, *-ation* The suffixes *-ion* and *-ation* turn a word into a noun. Look at the first row of the chart below to see how a new noun is built and defined. Fill in all the missing boxes in each row. Spelling changes will occur, so be sure to check spellings in a dictionary.

Word	+ Suffix *-ion* or *-ation*	Meaning of Noun
Example: *vary*	*variation*	*the act or process of changing*
calculate		the act of counting
		the act of gathering
	evaluation	
estimate		
	inflation	

Speak It! Give a weather forecast like a TV weather reporter. Make it silly or serious. Use as many words from this unit as you can.

Context Clues

for Word Wisdom

Choosing Work:

Taking Care of Animals

Have you thought about what kind of work you would like to do when you grow up? Learn about the real-life world of work by reading this article.

Do you love animals? Do you have an **aptitude** for understanding them and handling them? Then consider a **career** in animal care. Here are descriptions of a few careers that you may find rewarding.

The field of veterinary medicine is broad. Veterinarians are animal doctors. Some treat small animals, mostly pets. Some specialize in treating horses, cattle, and other large animals. Some veterinarians work in zoos or with animals in the wild. The **preparation** for a career in veterinary medicine begins with science courses in middle school and high school. Students then enroll in a four-year college with a science program that provides pre-vet training. After graduating from college, students apply to highly **competitive** veterinary medical schools for another four years of classroom lessons and hands-on experience. Lastly, they pass a difficult exam and are

licensed to practice. The average **salary** is fairly modest, but there are other **benefits,** like the satisfaction of helping animals.

A training program of two years or four years is required for a position as a veterinary **technician**. A technician assists in surgery and cares for animals under treatment. Some technicians work in animal hospital **management**.

Animal caretakers include groomers, who maintain the appearance of pets such as dogs and cats. Groomers generally get their training on the job, as **apprentices** to experienced workers. They may also attend grooming school and pass an examination.

To learn more about these careers, you can volunteer in animal shelters or nature centers. Set your own goals to **accomplish** your dreams. You may discover that you can put your love of animals to work for a lifetime.

Context Clues Strategy

Look for Words Related to the Word

EXAMPLE: Zookeepers care for zoo animals and sometimes serve as *surrogate* parents to newborn animals.

CLUE: The words *care for*, *parents*, and *newborn* help you make connections to the related word *surrogate*. You can make a good guess that *surrogate* means "substitute."

Use these steps to figure out the meaning of the word *aptitude* in the article about caring for animals.

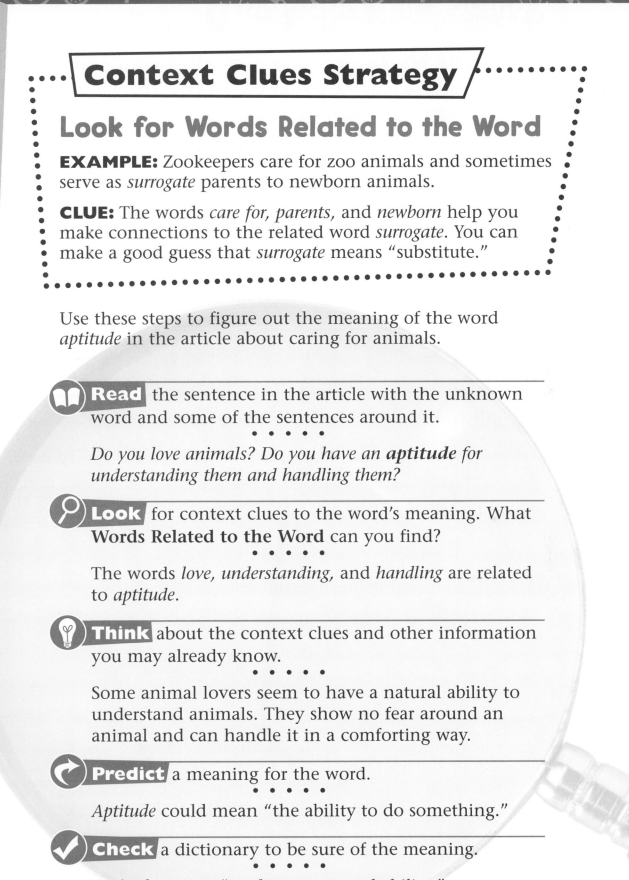

Read the sentence in the article with the unknown word and some of the sentences around it.

*Do you love animals? Do you have an **aptitude** for understanding them and handling them?*

Look for context clues to the word's meaning. What **Words Related to the Word** can you find?

The words *love, understanding,* and *handling* are related to *aptitude*.

Think about the context clues and other information you may already know.

Some animal lovers seem to have a natural ability to understand animals. They show no fear around an animal and can handle it in a comforting way.

Predict a meaning for the word.

Aptitude could mean "the ability to do something."

Check a dictionary to be sure of the meaning.

Aptitude means "a talent or natural ability."

Unlock the Meanings

Practice the Strategy One of the boldfaced words from the article on page 116 is in the box below. Use the context clues strategy on page 117 to figure out the meaning of the word.

benefits

📖 **Read** the sentence in the article that includes the word *benefits* and some of the sentences around it.

🔍 **Look** for context clues to the word's meaning. What **Words Related to the Word** can you find?

_____

_____

_____

💡 **Think** about the context clues. What other helpful information do you know?

_____

_____

_____

➡️ **Predict** a meaning for the word *benefit*.

_____

_____

_____

✔️ **Check** the Word Wisdom Dictionary to be sure of the meaning of *benefit*. Which of the meanings for the word *benefit* fits the context?

_____

_____

Use Context Clues   You have been introduced to two of the words from the article about caring for animals. These words are checked off in the Word List. In the first column below, write the other eight words from the Word List. In the second column predict a meaning for each word. Then look up the word in a dictionary and write the meaning in the third column.

Vocabulary Word	Your Prediction	Dictionary Says
1		
2		
3		
4		
5		
6		
7		
8		

Process the Meanings

WORD LIST

- aptitude
- career
- preparation
- competitive
- salary
- benefit
- technician
- management
- apprentice
- accomplish

Use the Words Correctly in Writing Rewrite each sentence in your own words using the word in parentheses.

1 The college gets thousands of applications but admits only a few students. (competitive)

_____

2 Colleges offer courses in running a business. (management)

_____

3 Charles paints well because he has a talent for art. (aptitude)

_____

4 Someone who likes fixing cars may choose to work in an automotive repair shop. (technician)

_____

5 List the goals you would like to reach. (accomplish)

_____

Choose the Correct Word Write the word from the Word List that belongs in each sentence.

6 The worker's _____ is paid twice a month.

7 The _____ earned no salary but got valuable instruction and practice.

8 Courses in science are important _____ for future doctors.

9 Doing satisfying work is one _____ of education.

10 Sophie is training for a _____ in veterinary medicine.

Apply What You've Learned

Give Examples Use what you've learned to list two examples that fit each category.

1 **competitive** events _____

2 things to do in **preparation** for a party _____

_____

3 what **technicians** do _____

4 things you have an **aptitude** for _____

_____

5 **careers** that interest you _____

_____

Demonstrate Word Knowledge Answer each question.

6 Why does an **apprentice** usually work with others?

_____

7 How do you feel when you **accomplish** what you hoped to do?

_____

8 What is a **benefit** of attending school?_____

_____

9 What professions might earn a large **salary**?_____

_____

10 How can you help with the **management** of your class?

_____

Write It! Write a paragraph about your dream career. Use as many words from the Part 1 Word List as you can.

PART 2

Latin Roots

for Word Wisdom

The U.S. Treasury:
Making Money

You ask your mom for a few dollars. She says, "Money doesn't grow on trees, you know!" Well, where *does* money come from?

It would be nice, but no, money doesn't grow on trees. Instead, it comes from the U.S. Treasury. Our money is made by a special part of the Treasury called the Bureau of Engraving and Printing (BEP). The BEP makes all U.S. paper money, but it does not make our coin money. The U.S. Mint has that job. The BEP did not **forfeit** this job to the U.S. Mint. The Mint was actually around first. It was created in 1792. The BEP was developed around 1861. Before then, people used only coins.

Even though it does not make coins, the BEP still has a lot to do. To **supplement** its responsibilities, the BEP prints U.S. postage stamps, government security papers, and White House documents. But its biggest job is to make paper money, or currency.

The department has an extremely **efficient** system for making sure U.S. currency is **plentiful** for Americans. It prints 37 million bills each day! Most of these bills replace old, ripped, or worn out bills. If you have a torn bill that is not **reparable,** the BEP might give you money for it. They collect unusable bills.

Paper money is actually made from a blend of cotton and linen, just like your socks and sports **apparel**! This fabric is stretched to make the special paper. In fact, money first looks like large sheets of paper. Most bills are printed thirty-two to a sheet before they are cut. The BEP has a special **apparatus** for each stage of the printing and cutting processes.

The BEP has **implemented** new strategies to prevent the success of **counterfeit** money. Every seven to ten years, the designs change. There are different colors in the fibers in the paper. There is very small print that can be read only with the use of a magnifier. The only people that **profit** from fake money are those who use it. Everyone else loses money.

Now that you know how money is made, you can go earn some for yourself! But be careful how you spend it—it's not an endless supply!

Practice the Context Clues Strategy Here is one of the boldfaced words from the essay on page 122. Use the context clues strategy you learned in Part 1 on page 117 to figure out the meaning of this word.

implemented

Read the sentence that uses the word *implemented*. Read some of the sentences around the word.

Look for context clues to the word's meaning. Can you find any **Words Related to the Word**?

_____

_____

_____

Think about the context clues. What other helpful information do you know?

_____

_____

_____

Predict a meaning for the word *implement*.

_____

_____

_____

Check your Word Wisdom Dictionary to be sure of the meaning of the word *implement*. Which of the meanings for *implement* fits the context?

_____

_____

_____

Unlock the Meanings

In this unit you will be studying three more Latin roots. These roots help form words that are related to the topic of work and money.

Latin Root: **feit, fic, fit**
meaning: to make, to do
English word: *benefit*
meaning: something that helps

Latin Root: **ple, pli**
meaning: fill, full, plenty
English word: *accomplish*
meaning: to fulfill or succeed

Latin Root: **pair, par**
meaning: to prepare, to put in order
English word: *preparation*
meaning: the act of preparing; readiness

WORD LIST

- forfeit
- supplement
- efficient
- plentiful
- reparable
- apparel
- apparatus
- implement
- counterfeit
- profit

Sort by Roots Find the roots you just learned in the Word List. Then write each word in the correct column. Think of other words you know that come from the same Latin roots. Write each one in the correct column.

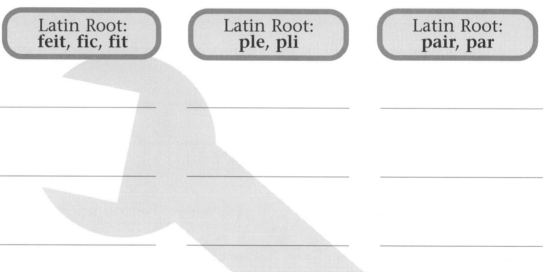

Latin Root: **feit, fic, fit**

Latin Root: **ple, pli**

Latin Root: **pair, par**

Work and Money

Prefix	Meaning
counter-	opposite
re-	back

Example

counter- (opposite) + **feit** (to make)
= **counterfeit**

Use Roots and Prefixes Circle the root and any prefix you find in each boldfaced word. Then use roots, prefixes, and context clues to write the meaning of each word. Check your definitions in a dictionary.

1 The odd color helped the bank clerk identify the **counterfeit** money.

_____

2 Because our team arrived too late, we had to **forfeit** the game.

_____

3 Marco was so **efficient** that he did all his homework before dinner.

_____

4 Scarves and mittens are appropriate **apparel** for cold winter weather.

_____

5 Since the squash in our garden was **plentiful**, we gave some to friends.

_____

6 The jeweler said that the broken antique watch was not **reparable**.

_____

7 Our teacher **implemented** a new system to teach us Spanish.

_____

8 Lily's braces are a metal **apparatus** for straightening teeth.

_____

9 People often take vitamins to **supplement** their diets.

_____

10 Her pet-sitting business made a **profit** because she had few costs.

_____

Process the Meanings

Complete the Analogies Write a word from the Word List to complete each analogy.

1 Stingy is to generous as scarce is to _____.

2 Chair is to furniture as shirt is to _____.

3 Outcome is to result as gain is to _____.

4 Strong is to weak as genuine is to _____.

Choose the Correct Meaning For each phrase below, write the word or phrase that gives the best meaning for the boldfaced word.

5 **apparatus** in the laboratory _____

    equipment   experiments   scientists

6 to **forfeit** privileges _____

    earn   give up   ask for

7 to **implement** a plan _____

    think of   put into action   improve upon

8 toys that are **reparable** _____

    able to be fixed   unable to be mended   able to be sold again

9 will **supplement** her salary _____

    spend   increase   add to

10 an **efficient** machine _____

    complicated   quiet   productive

Apply What You've Learned

Demonstrate Word Knowledge   Answer the questions below.

1 What **apparatus** might you find in a gym? _____

_____

2 Why would a boss want to hire **efficient** workers? _____

_____

3 How can a business increase its **profits**? _____

_____

4 What things in nature are becoming less **plentiful**? _____

_____

5 How might a teacher **supplement** information in your textbook?

_____

6 What kinds of **apparel** are you likely to see in the summer?

_____

7 What might you **forfeit** by not following your parents' rules?

_____

8 How can a mechanic show that a car is **reparable**?

_____

9 What would a police officer do to see if a check was **counterfeit**?

_____

10 What might happen if a builder's plans were poorly **implemented**?

_____

Speak It!   Give an oral report on a new business that has opened in your town. Use as many vocabulary words from Part 2 as possible.

PART 3

Reference Skills

for Word Wisdom

Career Study:

Banking

We all like money. It helps us do the things we want to do and buy the things we want to have. Well, when you grow up, why not get a job working with money?

We are all **amateur** bankers. We count our money, save it, and decide how to spend it. The difference between **professional** bankers and us is that they do these things for a living.

Banks help all kinds of people, from those with very little money to those who are quite **affluent**. As in most businesses, banks have **administrators**, or managers. These workers make sure that the bank runs smoothly. They handle problems, help special customers, and assign tasks to employees.

A bank has a lot of **personnel**. There are accountants, security guards, and bank tellers who handle everyday **transactions**. You might visit a teller to help you put money into your savings account.

A loan advisor is another bank employee. Say someone wants to buy a house. Usually, homes cost more money than what most people have in their savings accounts. A bank lets people borrow the money for this purchase. Then, over time, they pay back the money to the bank. Loan advisors help people decide which loan is right for them, and they make sure the bank lends money only to those people who will be able to pay it back.

These days, many banks have investment advisors. Their job is to help people **prosper** at banking. Investment advisors know just how to manage money in order to keep it safe and to make it grow. They can also help to prevent people from going **bankrupt**. These advisors help people to manage their money so that they will always be able to pay their bills.

Sometimes the names of banks change, even if the same people work there and little else changes. This often happens when two larger banks have a **merger**. When banks join together like this, they often become a better bank. The new bank keeps the best parts of both of the previous banks.

What do you want to be when you grow up? If you love money, think about becoming a banker. It is an exciting **enterprise,** and you will be able to help people with an important part of their lives—their money!

Practice the Context Clues Strategy   Here is one of the boldfaced words from the essay on page 128. Use the context clues strategy you learned in Part 1 on page 117 to figure out the meaning of this word.

personnel

Read the sentence that uses the word *personnel*. Read some of the sentences around the word.

Look for context clues. Can you find any **Words Related to the Word**?

_____

_____

 Think about the context clues. What other helpful information do you know?

_____

_____

Predict a meaning for the word *personnel*.

_____

_____

 Check your Word Wisdom Dictionary to be sure of the meaning of the word *personnel*. Write the definition here.

_____

_____

_____

Using a Thesaurus A thesaurus is a book that has useful information about words. Most word processing software also provides a thesaurus. A thesaurus entry often includes an entry word, a part of speech label, a definition, and a list of synonyms. Some entries also have antonyms. Read these three entries for the word *rich*.

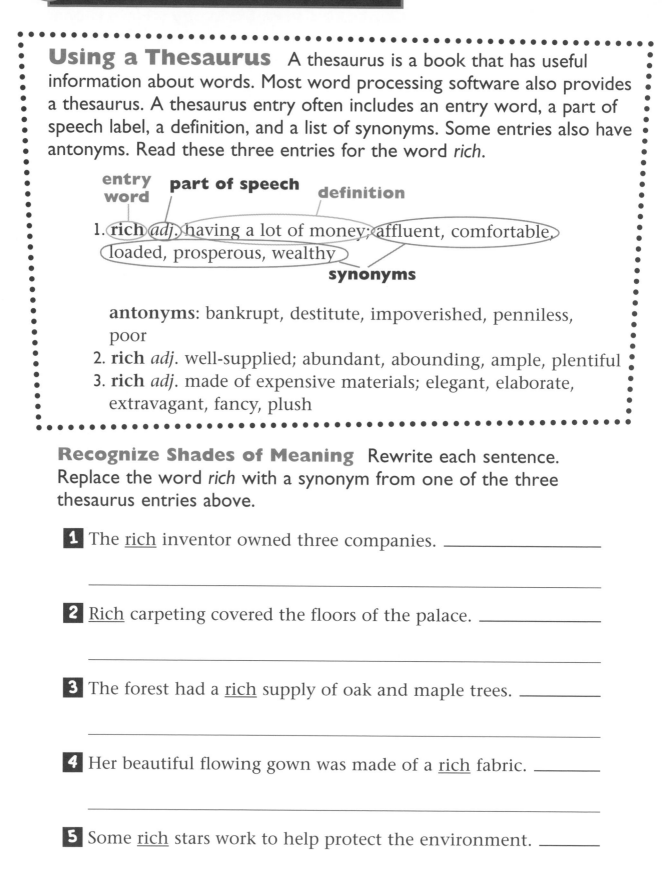

entry word **part of speech** **definition**

1. **rich** *adj.* having a lot of money; affluent, comfortable, loaded, prosperous, wealthy

synonyms

antonyms: bankrupt, destitute, impoverished, penniless, poor

2. **rich** *adj.* well-supplied; abundant, abounding, ample, plentiful
3. **rich** *adj.* made of expensive materials; elegant, elaborate, extravagant, fancy, plush

Recognize Shades of Meaning Rewrite each sentence. Replace the word *rich* with a synonym from one of the three thesaurus entries above.

1 The <u>rich</u> inventor owned three companies. _____

_____

2 <u>Rich</u> carpeting covered the floors of the palace. _____

_____

3 The forest had a <u>rich</u> supply of oak and maple trees. _____

_____

4 Her beautiful flowing gown was made of a <u>rich</u> fabric. _____

_____

5 Some <u>rich</u> stars work to help protect the environment. _____

_____

1. Use context clues.

2. Look for a familiar root, prefix, or suffix.

3. If the context or a word part doesn't help, check the dictionary.

Define the Words Follow the steps above to write the meaning of each boldfaced word. Write 1, 2, or 3 to show which steps you used.

WORD LIST

amateur

professional

affluent

administrator

personnel

transaction

prosper

bankrupt

merger

enterprise

1 Rasheen, an **amateur** golfer, plays the game on weekends.

_____

2 The **administrators** met to decide on next year's plan.

_____

3 She lost her job when her company went **bankrupt**.

_____

4 Digging the tunnel under the river was an enormous **enterprise**.

_____

5 The **affluent** family lived in a mansion by the ocean.

_____

6 All of the hotel's **personnel** were helpful and friendly to the guests.

_____

7 Akira is a **professional** musician whose new CD is now in stores.

_____

8 The **merger** of two small banks resulted in one larger corporation.

_____

9 I completed the business **transaction** by signing a contract.

_____

10 A talented chef will help the new restaurant **prosper**.

_____

Process the Meanings

WORD LIST

- amateur
- professional
- affluent
- administrator
- personnel
- transaction
- prosper
- bankrupt
- merger
- enterprise

Match the Antonyms Match each vocabulary word with its antonym. Write your answer on the line.

Vocabulary Word	Antonym
1 affluent _____	wealthy
2 prosper _____	poor
3 bankrupt _____	split
4 merger _____	fail

Choose the Correct Word Write the correct word from the Word List to complete each sentence.

5 Ani, a _____ writer, sells her articles to a magazine.

6 The company's top _____ was responsible for hiring staff.

7 Miriam's next _____ is to write a new musical about dogs.

8 The store clerk wrote each _____ in a record book.

9 Our counselors and other camp _____ emphasize safety rules.

10 Like many _____ photographers, Jed takes his camera everywhere.

Apply What You've Learned

Find Examples Read each description. Then put a check beside every example that matches the description.

1 signs that a town is **affluent**
- ☐ fancy houses
- ☐ expensive cars
- ☐ lots of trees
- ☐ young people

2 kinds of **personnel**
- ☐ nurses in a hospital
- ☐ tellers in a bank
- ☐ students in a school
- ☐ parents in an audience

3 usual jobs for an **administrator**
- ☐ organizing projects
- ☐ cleaning the office
- ☐ explaining tasks to workers
- ☐ buying supplies

4 kinds of business **transactions**
- ☐ going to work
- ☐ selling a house
- ☐ copying a contract
- ☐ paying for groceries

5 activities of an **amateur** baseball player
- ☐ playing for fun
- ☐ getting paid to pitch
- ☐ signing a contract with a team
- ☐ playing in a weekend league

6 ways companies go **bankrupt**
- ☐ selling good products
- ☐ making poor products
- ☐ investing badly
- ☐ wasting money

Complete the Analogies Write a word from the Word List to complete each analogy.

7 Person is to marriage as company is to _____.

8 Apprentice is to expert as unskilled is to _____.

9 Limit is to restrict as succeed is to _____.

10 Action is to performance as project is to _____.

Write It! Write some headlines that might appear in the business section of a magazine or a newspaper. Use as many words from Part 3 as possible.

PART 4

Review

for Word Wisdom

Replace Words Read each business news headline below. Choose words from the Word List that could replace the underlined word and still make sense. Write them in each section. The numbers tell how many words to list.

WORD LIST

- aptitude
- career
- preparation
- competitive
- salary
- benefit
- technician
- management
- apprentice
- accomplish
- forfeit
- supplement
- efficient
- plentiful
- reparable
- apparel
- apparatus
- implement
- counterfeit
- profit
- amateur
- professional
- affluent
- administrator
- personnel
- transaction
- prosper
- bankrupt
- merger
- enterprise

This Person Loves Her Job (5)

Store Owner Has Plans to Grow (2)

Advertisers Set New Goals (2)

Company Seeks Workers Who Have the Right Skill for the Job (2)

Business Move Surprises Everyone (10)

Choose One of Two Read each sentence and the two words in parentheses. Circle the word that completes the sentence correctly.

1 He took a second job in order to ____ his income. (supplement , forfeit)

2 MoneySave Bank and MoreMoney Bank became SaveMoreMoney Bank after the ____. (supplement, merger)

3 Subtract your costs from your earnings to find your ____. (apparatus, profit)

4 Doctors, editors, and engineers are ____ workers. (professional, amateur)

5 If the car is ____, we should have it towed to the shop. (apparatus, reparable)

Check the Meanings If the boldfaced word is used **Correctly,** write **C**. If it is used **Incorrectly,** write **I**. On the line, briefly explain the reason for your choice.

____ **6** Some things are too **personnel** to tell strangers. _____

_____

____ **7** Business owners hope to **prosper**. _____

_____

____ **8** A negative **aptitude** might affect your health. _____

_____

____ **9** When jobs are **plentiful**, workers are pleased. _____

_____

____ **10** Mrs. Pierre has a successful **career** in real estate. _____

_____

Taking Vocabulary Tests

Some vocabulary tests ask you to choose a synonym for a word in a sentence. The correct answer will closely match the meaning of the word in the test sentence. Look over the answer choices. You will probably find other words that make sense in the sentence or that are close to the meaning of the word. Don't be fooled! Study all of the choices before deciding on the correct answer.

Sample:

Fill in the letter by the answer that has the SAME or ALMOST THE SAME meaning as the boldfaced word.

The **veterinarian** saved the puppy's life.

Ⓐ animal control officer
Ⓑ animal doctor
Ⓒ animal trainer
Ⓓ animal breeder

Practice Test Fill in the letter by the answer that has the SAME or ALMOST THE SAME meaning as the boldfaced word.

1 Nadia **accomplished** her goals.
Ⓐ set
Ⓑ helped
Ⓒ fulfilled
Ⓓ changed

2 The successful **management** of a large business takes skill.
Ⓐ products
Ⓑ supervision
Ⓒ customers
Ⓓ effort

3 This money is **counterfeit**.
Ⓐ fake
Ⓑ useless
Ⓒ useful
Ⓓ odd

4 The **salary** was paid.
Ⓐ tax
Ⓑ loan
Ⓒ wage
Ⓓ salesperson

5 The **administrator** is in her office.
Ⓐ supervisor
Ⓑ clerk
Ⓒ doctor
Ⓓ lawyer

6 Complete the business **transaction**.
Ⓐ construction
Ⓑ meeting
Ⓒ agreement
Ⓓ dispute

7 Set up the **apparatus** for the experiment.
Ⓐ chemicals
Ⓑ notebook
Ⓒ ingredients
Ⓓ equipment

8 We'll find women's **apparel** at the mall.
Ⓐ businesses
Ⓑ shoes
Ⓒ dresses
Ⓓ clothing

9 The artist has three **apprentices**.
Ⓐ trainees
Ⓑ workshops
Ⓒ paintings
Ⓓ managers

10 The town has **affluent** people.
Ⓐ large
Ⓑ rich
Ⓒ friendly
Ⓓ two-language

Missing-Letter Synonyms Write the missing letters of a common synonym for the word from the Word List. Use a thesaurus if you need help. Write one letter in each box.

Word List	Synonyms
1 enterprise	[ ] [ ] [o] [j] [e] [ ] [t]
2 bankrupt	[ ] [ ] [i] [n]
3 prospers	[g] [ ] [ ] [w] [ ]
4 implement	[ ] [s] [ ]
5 efficient	[ ] [a] [n] [d] [ ]
6 forfeit	[l] [ ] [ ] [e]
7 merger	[ ] [i] [x] [t] [ ] [ ] [e]
8 apparel	[ ] [ ] [ ] [s] [s]
9 benefit	[ ] [d] [v] [a] [n] [ ] [a] [g] [e]
10 competitive	[ ] [a] [t] [c] [ ] [e] [d]

Write the shaded letters in order. You will find the answer to this question: *What is good career advice for a young person?*

— — — — — — —   — — — —   — — — — —

Speak It! Choose a partner and role-play a reporter interviewing a business owner. Ask questions about the business and its plans for the future. Use several vocabulary words from this unit.

Context Clues

for Word Wisdom

Reading About Writing:
A Book Review

How do you choose a book to read for pleasure? You might ask a friend or a librarian for a recommendation. Or you might read a book review like this one.

Authors of great **literature** explore ideas that matter to everyone. They create stories about friendship, love, loyalty, honesty, trust, respect, guilt, punishment, and other themes. All of these ideas are in a book I would like to recommend to young readers. The book is *The Real Thief*, by the author-illustrator William Steig. William Steig's well-known and **esteemed** picture books for children include *Sylvester and the Magic Pebble, Doctor De Soto*, and *Shrek!* Although Steig drew illustrations for *The Real Thief*, it is not a picture book. The cartoon-style drawings are entertaining, but the book presents serious themes, not **comical** ones. It was written for children, but it is **sophisticated** enough for adults to enjoy.

Because of its animal characters, *The Real Thief* has the flavor of **folklore**. Gawain the goose guards the Royal Treasury of King Basil, a bear. Gawain loves the fatherly king and serves him with pride and loyalty. A **crisis** arises when treasure disappears from the Royal Treasury. Gawain is accused of the theft, tried in court, and found guilty. He escapes before being imprisoned and hides in the woods. Gawain's friend, Derek the mouse, is the real thief. Derek decides to take action to clear his friend's name. By the end of the story, all of the characters have learned to forgive one another.

This plot summary barely hints at Steig's masterly **depiction** of the characters' troubles. The author shows Gawain's hurt and anger. Readers see why the shame-filled Derek does not confess and help his friend. The book is filled with moving and **graphic** descriptions of the characters' thoughts and feelings.

One reason that Steig's books appeal to children is that even when his story has a "lesson," it never **plods** along. Steig's writing is sharp and **brilliant**. *The Real Thief* is a gem. I highly recommend it!

Context Clues Strategy

Look for Words That Mean the Opposite

EXAMPLE: The writer showed respect for his readers' intelligence by using a *voluminous* vocabulary instead of simple words.

CLUE: The words *instead of* are a clue. The phrase *simple words* is the opposite of *voluminous*. A *voluminous* vocabulary is large and advanced.

Here is another strategy for using context clues. Use it here to understand the meaning of the word *comical* from the book review.

Read the sentence with the unknown word and some of the sentences around it.

*The cartoon-style drawings are entertaining, but the book presents serious themes, not **comical** ones.*

Look for context clues. What **Words That Mean the Opposite** can you find?

The word *serious* means the opposite of *comical*.

Think about the context clues and other information you may already know.

Serious things are not funny. The word *comic* is in *comical*. The comics in a newspaper are funny.

Predict a meaning for the word.

The word *comical* probably means "funny and entertaining."

Check the Word Wisdom Dictionary to be sure of the meaning.

The word *comical* means "funny."

Unlock the Meanings

Practice the Strategy Here is one of the boldfaced words from the book review on page 138. Use the context clues strategy on page 139 to figure out the meaning of the word.

sophisticated

Read the sentence that uses the word *sophisticated* and some of the sentences around it.

Look for context clues to the word's meaning. What **Words That Mean the Opposite** can you find?

_____

_____

_____

Think about the context clues. What other helpful information do you know?

_____

_____

_____

Predict a meaning for the word *sophisticated*.

_____

_____

Check the Word Wisdom Dictionary to be sure of the meaning of *sophisticated*. Decide which meaning fits the context.

_____

_____

Use Context Clues Two words you have learned from the book review are checked off in the Word List. In the first column, write the other eight words from the Word List. In the second column, use context clues to predict a meaning for each word. Then look up the word in the Word Wisdom Dictionary. In the third column, write the dictionary meaning that fits the context.

WORD LIST

literature

esteemed

✔ comical

✔ sophisticated

folklore

crisis

depiction

graphic

plod

brilliant

	Vocabulary Word	Your Prediction	Dictionary Says
1			
2			
3			
4			
5			
6			
7			
8			

Process the Meanings

WORD LIST

literature

esteemed

comical

sophisticated

folklore

crisis

depiction

graphic

plod

brilliant

Find Synonyms Write the word from the Word List that is a synonym for the boldfaced word in each sentence. You will need to add an ending to one word.

1 Please welcome our **admired** speaker, who will read from her book. _____

2 The author's **description** of the family was believable. _____

3 His dull but steady work **drudged** along. _____

4 What a **smart** idea you came up with, you genius! _____

5 Everyone giggled at Aisha's **amusing** facial expression. _____

6 Trevor is too **mature** to believe everything he hears. _____

Choose the Correct Word Write the word from the Word List that completes each sentence.

7 *Charlotte's Web* by E. B. White is a classic of children's

_____.

8 I love legends, myths, and _____.

9 Readers feel as if they are in the storm because the description

is so _____.

10 I couldn't wait to find out how the characters managed the

difficult _____.

Apply What You've Learned

Add Examples   Use what you have learned to add the
vocabulary word that belongs in each group.

1 humorous, clownish, silly, _____

2 danger, emergency, moment of truth, _____

3 sculpture, music, dance, _____

4 customs, beliefs, holidays, _____

5 experienced, knowledgeable, grown-up, _____

Demonstrate Word Knowledge   Answer each question.

6 Do you enjoy reading books that have **depictions** of people
your age? Why or why not?

_____

7 What are **brilliant** students expected to do?

_____

8 What is something that seems to **plod** along for you?

_____

9 What well-known person do you think should be **esteemed**?
Why?

_____

10 Would you like to read a **graphic** account of a roller coaster
ride? Why or why not?

_____

Write It!   Write your own book review. Try to get
readers interested in the book you are writing about. Use
as many vocabulary words from Part 1 as you can.

PART 2

Latin and Greek Roots

for Word Wisdom

It's All in the Family:
The Brontë Sisters

Charlotte, Emily, and Anne Brontë were English writers who lived in the 1800s. Some people think that their short lives were as interesting as their stories.

The Brontë sisters truly loved literature. They dreamed of being published authors someday. Sadly, none of them lived long enough to see how admired their writing would become. Remember the **acronym** *CEA*. It sounds like *sea* and can help you remember the order in which the sisters were born: *Charlotte* (1816), *Emily* (1818), and *Anne* (1820).

Each of the Brontë sisters took a **pseudonym**. Charlotte wrote under the name Currer Bell; Emily was Ellis Bell; and Anne was Acton Bell. Together, they published a book of poems called *Poems by Currer, Ellis, and Acton Bell*. Later, Charlotte explained why the sisters used men's names: "…we did not like to declare ourselves as women, because … authoresses are [likely] to be looked on with prejudice."

Fans of the Brontës are glad their writing was not **anonymous**. We may have never known who these sisters were!

The Brontë sisters were very **literate** children. They wrote many stories about made-up worlds. They continued to write as they grew up. This was a time before typewriters, so the sisters' poems and novels were written by hand. The British Library in England has a sample page from Charlotte's novel *Jane Eyre*. You can see her beautiful writing style. It looks like fancy **calligraphy**!

In their poetry, the sisters experimented with language. They used **alliteration**. They played with **homonyms**. As with all poetry, you must look beyond the **literal** meaning of the words to truly understand these poems.

If you want to learn more about the Brontës, find a **bibliography** of resources on their lives and works. None of the sisters wrote the story of her own life. But the writer Elizabeth Gaskell wrote Charlotte's **biography**. This book is a great place to start.

Practice the Context Clues Strategy   Here is one of the boldfaced words from the essay on page 144. Use the context clues strategy you learned in Part 1 on page 139 to figure out the meaning of this word.

pseudonym

 Read the sentence that uses the word *pseudonym*. Read some of the sentences around the word.

 Look for context clues to the word's meaning. Can you find any **Words That Mean the Opposite** of the word?

_____

_____

_____

Think about the context clues. What other helpful information do you know?

_____

_____

_____

Predict a meaning for the word *pseudonym*.

_____

_____

_____

 Check your Word Wisdom Dictionary to be sure of the meaning of the word *pseudonym*. Write the definition here.

_____

_____

_____

🔑 Unlock the Meanings

In this unit you will learn one Latin root and two Greek roots that are related to language and writing. Knowing these roots will help you recognize many English words and learn their meanings.

Latin Root: **litera** meaning: letter English word: *literature* meaning: writing that is of lasting value	Greek Root: **graph** meaning: to write English word: *graphic* meaning: described in clear detail	Greek Root: **nym** meaning: name English word: *antonym* meaning: a word having the opposite meaning

WORD LIST

- acronym
- pseudonym
- anonymous
- literate
- calligraphy
- alliteration
- homonym
- literal
- bibliography
- biography

Sort by Roots Find the roots you just learned in the Word List. Then write each word in the correct column. Think of other words you know that come from the same Latin and Greek roots. Write each one in the correct column.

Latin Root: **litera**	Greek Root: **graph**	Greek Root: **nym**

Language and Writing

Prefix	Meaning
bio-	life
pseudo-	false

Example

bio- (life) + graph (write) + -y (noun) = biography

Use Roots and Prefixes Circle the root and any prefix you find in each boldfaced word. Use context clues, roots, and prefixes to write the meaning of each word. Check your definitions in a dictionary.

1 This **biography** of Roberto Clemente tells facts about his life.

_____

2 Mary Evans used the **pseudonym** George Eliot, not her real name.

_____

3 Nick listed the books he used in a **bibliography** at the end of his report.

_____

4 "Roaring, raging river" is one example of **alliteration**.

_____

5 The **acronym** RADAR stands for "radio detecting and ranging."

_____

6 The wedding invitations were written in **calligraphy**.

_____

7 Our teacher explained the **literal** meaning of the poem.

_____

8 The words *scene* and *seen* are **homonyms**.

_____

9 If people are **literate**, they can read newspapers and write letters.

_____

10 No one at school knew who had written the **anonymous** note.

_____

Process the Meanings

WORD LIST

- acronym
- pseudonym
- anonymous
- literate
- calligraphy
- alliteration
- homonym
- literal
- bibliography
- biography

Match the Examples Match each example to the vocabulary word it represents. Write the word on the line.

Example	Vocabulary Word
1 *Eleanor Roosevelt: A Life of Discovery*	acronym
2 large, leaping leopard	biography
3 Samuel Clemens, also known as Mark Twain	calligraphy
4 NASA is the National Aeronautics and Space Administration.	pseudonym
5 *beautiful* writing	alliteration

Revise Sentences Rewrite each sentence. Replace the underlined words with a word from the Word List. You may have to add an ending.

6 At the back of the book is a <u>list of sources</u>. _____

_____

7 If you're not <u>able to read and write</u>, you won't get a good job.

_____

8 To stay <u>unknown</u>, she didn't give her name. _____

_____

9 The words *sail* and *sale* <u>sound the same but have different meanings and spellings</u>.

_____

10 He gave a <u>factual</u> explanation of the character's actions.

_____

Apply What You've Learned

Give Examples Use what you know about the boldfaced words to write an example of each item.

1 words that are **homonyms** _____

2 a favorite **biography** _____

3 **alliteration** with the letter *m* _____

4 an **acronym** and its meaning _____

5 a place you might see **calligraphy** _____

Name the Categories Write a word from the Word List to complete each category. Tell what category the words belong to.

6 educated, scholarly, _____

Category: _____

7 table of contents, index, _____

Category: _____

8 title, nickname, _____

Category: _____

9 accurate, precise, _____

Category: _____

10 unidentified, hidden, _____

Category: _____

Speak It! Imagine that you have written a book about a person that you admire. Tell a friend about your book. Use several vocabulary words from Part 2.

PART 3

Reference Skills

for Word Wisdom

A New Debate:
Music As Literature?

Do you believe that music is a form of literature? Some people argue that it is, while others disagree. Read this article to learn more about musical lyrics.

There are two sides to every argument. But this **document** will only present one side of the music-as-literature debate: Music should be considered one of the many **genres** of literature. After all, music is **published** just as other literature is. Like literature, music is a form of expression. Also, you can hear a sample of a song on the Internet just as you can read an **excerpt** of a novel. Some song lyrics, or the words to a song, are complete **fiction** while others tell about the writer's real life or ideas; the same is true of literature.

Song lyrics are most commonly compared to poetry. They have a style and a structure similar to poetry. And song lyrics use many elements that poems use, such as rhythm, rhyme, and **figurative** language.

Some of a song's rhythm comes from musical instruments, but it can also come from its lyrics. To create rhythm, a writer chooses just the right mix of **syllables** for each line. He or she chooses a song's words very carefully. And, as in poetry, rhyme is used to make the song flow smoothly.

A **simile** is one example of figurative language. Similes use the words *like* or *as* to compare things that do not seem to be related. Song lyrics often use similes. For example, a well-known song by Simon & Garfunkel includes the simile "like a bridge over troubled water" to describe friendship. Song lyrics also use other writing tools, such as **idioms**. You may have heard the song "Walking on Sunshine" by the group Me First & the Gimme Gimmes. No one is *actually* walking on sunshine! It is an idiom.

Some writers are influenced by literature they have read. In the same way, musicians are influenced by other music, especially by that of earlier generations. To show this strong influence, some musicians might perform a cover, or their own **version** of someone else's song.

These are just a few of the ways in which music is similar to literature. But for some people, this is enough! What about you? Do you think music should be considered a kind of literature?

Practice the Context Clues Strategy Here is one of the boldfaced words from the essay on page 150. Use the context clues strategy you learned in Part 1 on page 139 to figure out the meaning of this word.

fiction

 Read the sentence that uses the word *fiction*. Read some of the sentences around the word.

 Look for context clues to the word's meaning. Can you find any **Words That Mean the Opposite**?

_____

_____

_____

 Think about the context clues. What other helpful information do you know?

_____

_____

_____

Predict a meaning for the word *fiction*.

_____

_____

_____

Check your Word Wisdom Dictionary to be sure of the meaning of the word *fiction*. Write the definition here.

_____

_____

_____

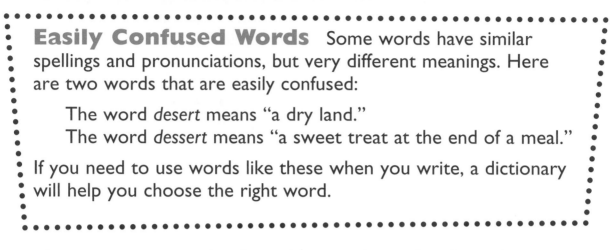

Unlock the Meanings

Easily Confused Words Some words have similar spellings and pronunciations, but very different meanings. Here are two words that are easily confused:

The word *desert* means "a dry land."
The word *dessert* means "a sweet treat at the end of a meal."

If you need to use words like these when you write, a dictionary will help you choose the right word.

Find and Define Look up these easily confused words in a dictionary. Write their meanings in your own words.

1 fiction   _____

2 friction   _____

3 conscious   _____

4 conscience   _____

5 except   _____

6 excerpt   _____

7 access   _____

8 excess   _____

9 formally   _____

10 formerly   _____

Find the Meaning

1. Use context clues.
2. Look for a familiar root, prefix, or suffix.
3. If the context or a word part doesn't help, check the dictionary.

Define the Words Follow the steps above to write the meaning of each boldfaced word. Write 1, 2, or 3 to show which steps you used.

WORD LIST

document
genre
publish
excerpt
fiction
figurative
syllable
simile
idiom
version

1 Ramin's story will be **published** in a children's magazine.

_____

2 An **excerpt**, not the entire interview, appeared in the newspaper.

_____

3 Science fiction is Mabel's favorite **genre** of literature.

_____

4 The new **version** of the play had more jokes than the original did.

_____

5 She used the **simile** "as cold as ice" to describe how her toes felt.

_____

6 The Declaration of Independence is a historical **document**.

_____

7 The use of **figurative** language made the description vivid.

_____

8 The first **syllable** in *mystery* is *mys*.

_____

9 He enjoys reading **fiction** rather than informational books.

_____

10 The **idiom** "raining cats and dogs" isn't about pets.

_____

Process the Meanings

WORD LIST

- document
- genre
- publish
- excerpt
- fiction
- figurative
- syllable
- simile
- idiom
- version

Solve the Riddles Write a word from the Word List for each clue.

1 It's a part of a word. _____

2 Short stories and poetry are two examples of this.

_____

3 Your report card is an important one. _____

4 It can be a few sentences from an article.

_____

5 "Roaring with laughter" is an example of this kind of

language. _____

6 It's a story about people who never existed.

_____

Choose the Correct Words Write the correct word from the Word List to complete each sentence.

7 "Hold your horses" is a(n) _____ that

means "be patient."

8 Daniel will _____ a collection of songs

that he has composed.

9 I wrote a(n) _____ comparing my

brother's cough to the sound of thunder.

10 I wonder if the new _____ of the movie

is better than the old one.

Apply What You've Learned

Complete the Analogies Choose the correct word to complete each analogy. Write the word on the line.

1 Sofa is to couch as **excerpt** is to _____ .
   book   reading   passage   author

2 Nonfiction is to essay as **fiction** is to _____ .
   story   movie   chapter   index

3 Periodical is to magazine as **genre** is to _____ .
   phrase   myth   library   vocabulary

4 Literal is to factual as **figurative** is to _____ .
   beautiful   harmful   dangerous   imaginative

5 Perform is to actor as **publish** is to _____ .
   teacher   author   banker   pilot

6 Scene is to play as **syllable** is to _____ .
   word   paragraph   page   sentence

Demonstrate Word Knowledge Answer each question.

7 Why might someone not understand an **idiom**?

_____

8 Why might there be two different **versions** of the same song?

_____

9 Write a **simile** about how busy you are.

_____

10 What **document** will you get when you graduate from school?

_____

Write It! Write information about your favorite book or its author for a book jacket. Use as many vocabulary words from Part 3 as you can.

Review
for Word Wisdom

WORD LIST

literature
esteemed
comical
sophisticated
folklore
crisis
depiction
graphic
plod
brilliant
acronym
pseudonym
anonymous
literate
calligraphy
alliteration
homonym
literal
bibliography
biography
document
genre
publish
excerpt
fiction
figurative
syllable
simile
idiom
version

Sort the Librarian's Words Read the words spoken by a helpful librarian. Choose vocabulary words that make sense in the blank, and list them below the librarian's words. The numbers tell you how many words to list.

A Librarian's Words

"Do you want to read informational books, or do you prefer _____?" ③

"I enjoyed this story by a(n) _____ author, and you might like it too." ⑥

"Does this book contain the _____ you need for your report?" ④

"I will read aloud the poem 'As Sneaky as a Snake.' Do you like the _____ in the title?" ②

Label the Examples Read each example. Write the letter of the answer that is the best label for the boldfaced part of each example.

Example	Label
_____ **1** **OPEC, the Organization of Petroleum Exporting Countries**	a. a simile
_____ **2** The afternoon was **as hot as an oven**.	b. a biography
_____ **3** **deer** and **dear**	c. an acronym
_____ **4** With nothing to do, we were soon **climbing the walls**.	d. homonyms
_____ **5** *The Daring Nellie Bly: America's Star Reporter*, written and illustrated by Bonnie Christensen	e. an idiom
_____ **6** Charlotte Brontë, also known as **Currer Bell**	f. a pseudonym

Answer True or False Read each statement. Decide whether it is true or false, and circle **T** or **F** to show your choice. Then write your reason on the line.

7 The word *potato* has two **syllables**.   T   F

_____

8 Mystery stories are a **genre**.   T   F

_____

9 During a **crisis**, people often feel bored.   T   F

_____

10 Skilled musicians usually perform **calligraphy**.   T   F

_____

Taking Vocabulary Tests

When you are taking a timed test, start by looking over the whole test. See how many sections there are, and decide whether some sections will take longer to complete than others. If you are stumped on a question, skip it and move on. Always do the easy questions first. That way, you will get credit for what you do know. If time allows, go back to figure out the items you skipped.

Sample:

Fill in the letter of the answer that has the SAME or ALMOST THE SAME meaning as the boldfaced word.

the story's **theme**

- Ⓐ characters
- Ⓑ setting
- Ⓒ plot
- Ⓓ main idea

Practice Test Fill in the letter of the answer that has the SAME or ALMOST THE SAME meaning as the boldfaced word.

1 a **graphic** description
- Ⓐ numbered
- Ⓑ lengthy and dull
- Ⓒ handwritten
- Ⓓ clear and detailed

2 an up-to-date **version**
- Ⓐ reference book
- Ⓑ edition
- Ⓒ poem
- Ⓓ machine

3 the **esteemed** visitor
- Ⓐ respected
- Ⓑ delayed
- Ⓒ friendly
- Ⓓ unwelcome

4 to **publish** the book
- Ⓐ purchase
- Ⓑ proofread
- Ⓒ borrow
- Ⓓ print for sale

5 **figurative** language
- Ⓐ literal
- Ⓑ competitive
- Ⓒ creative
- Ⓓ spoken

6 a **literal** translation
- Ⓐ word-for-word
- Ⓑ figurative
- Ⓒ creative
- Ⓓ well-written

7 **plod** along
- Ⓐ rush
- Ⓑ help
- Ⓒ move slowly
- Ⓓ speed

8 write a **bibliography**
- Ⓐ story of someone's life
- Ⓑ story of one's own life
- Ⓒ list of sources
- Ⓓ book review

9 read the **excerpt**
- Ⓐ professional advice
- Ⓑ selection from a written work
- Ⓒ answer
- Ⓓ essay

10 **depictions** of life long ago
- Ⓐ memories
- Ⓑ proof
- Ⓒ descriptions
- Ⓓ diaries

Build New Words

Add Suffixes Add suffixes as shown to write a new word. Use your dictionary to check the new word spellings. Then think about the meaning of the new word as you read the sentences below. Write the correct word to complete each sentence.

Word	+ Suffix	+ Suffix	= New Word
fiction	+ -al		
document	+ -ary		
idiom	+ -atic		
syllable	+ -ic	+ -ate	
biography	+ -ic	+ -al	

1 Certain _____ expressions like "fly off the handle" are hard to explain.

2 I read a(n) _____ article about the scientist Rachel Carson.

3 The filmmaker's _____ shows a visit to China.

4 Draw three lines to _____ the word *education*.

5 The short story is based on fact, but it is mainly a(n) _____ work.

Speak It! Folklore is made up of stories passed down over many years, so there can be many versions of the same story. Tell a familiar story to the class, but make a small change. See if your classmates can catch the change.

PART
1

Context Clues

for Word Wisdom

Human Rights:
Eleanor Roosevelt

After World War II ended in 1945, Eleanor Roosevelt, the widow of U.S. President Franklin Roosevelt, had hope for a better world.

Legal Matters

UNIT 8

When World War II ended, many people wanted a new organization called the United Nations to be a **forum** for peaceful discussions. World leaders could meet to **resolve** conflicts before those conflicts exploded into war.

Nations sent **delegates,** or official agents, to meetings to plan the United Nations (UN). Eleanor Roosevelt was among the delegates representing the United States. "If we wish, we can destroy ourselves and our entire civilization," she pointed out. "If we do not wish to do this, then we must learn to get on together without war."

Eleanor Roosevelt had earned respect for her tireless work for **humanitarian** causes. As a result, she was elected to lead the UN Human Rights Commission. The Commission was supposed to establish a bill of rights for the world.

The Commission delegates came from eighteen nations. They disagreed about how to **codify,** or put

into the language of law, ideas such as freedom and **justice**. Eleanor Roosevelt worked hard to overcome **protests**. The document had to be acceptable to everyone. Yet she wanted it to recognize that all people "were born free and equal in **dignity** and rights." The **negotiations** lasted for nearly three years.

The member nations of the UN adopted the Universal Declaration of Human Rights in late 1948. Its thirty Articles set forth basic freedoms for "all peoples and all nations." These rights include life, liberty, security, privacy, ownership of property, education, and freedom to travel and live where one wishes. Everyone is entitled to equal treatment under the law. Anyone accused of a crime has the right to a fair and public hearing by an independent **tribunal**.

Eleanor Roosevelt considered the Universal Declaration of Human Rights—the hope for a better world—her highest achievement.

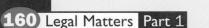

Context Clues Strategy

Look for Words That Mean the Same

EXAMPLE: Eleanor Roosevelt was a strong **advocate**, or supporter, of human rights.

CLUE: The phrase *or supporter* is set between commas after the word and is a synonym for *advocate*.

Here are the steps for using this context clues strategy to figure out the meaning of the word *delegates*.

Read the sentence with the unknown word and some of the sentences around it.

*Nations sent **delegates**, or official agents, to meetings to plan the United Nations (UN). Eleanor Roosevelt was among the delegates representing the United States.*

Look for context clues to the word's meaning. What **Words That Mean the Same** can you find?

The words *or official agents* are set between commas after *delegates*. This may be a definition for *delegates*.

Think about the context clues and other information you may already know.

The U.S. was one of the nations sending official agents to meetings. Eleanor Roosevelt was an agent.

Predict a meaning for the word *delegates*.

Delegate could mean "an official agent at a meeting; someone who represents a large group."

Check your Word Wisdom Dictionary to be sure of the meaning.

Delegate means "a person chosen to speak or act for others; representative."

Practice the Strategy One of the boldfaced words from the article on page 160 is in the box below. Use the context clues strategy on page 161 to figure out the meaning of the word.

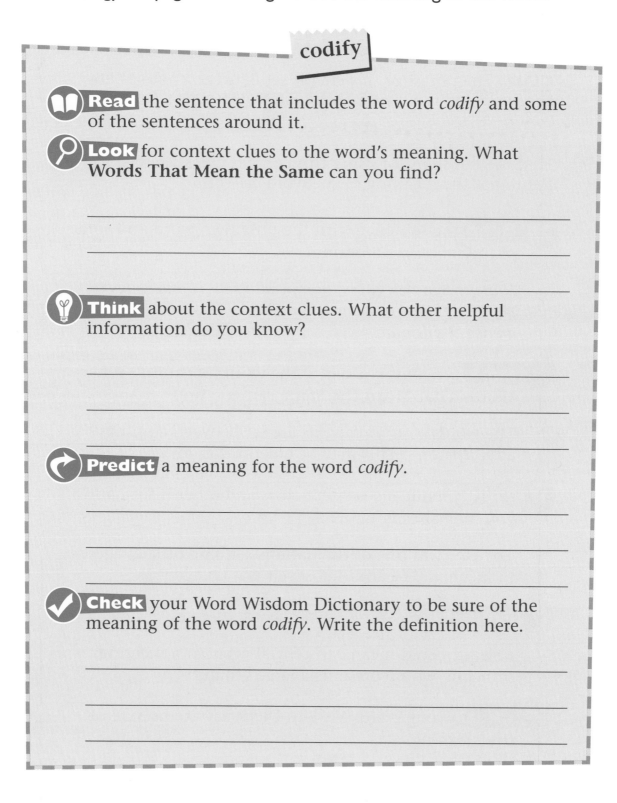

codify

Read the sentence that includes the word *codify* and some of the sentences around it.

Look for context clues to the word's meaning. What **Words That Mean the Same** can you find?

_____

_____

_____

Think about the context clues. What other helpful information do you know?

_____

_____

_____

Predict a meaning for the word *codify*.

_____

_____

_____

Check your Word Wisdom Dictionary to be sure of the meaning of the word *codify*. Write the definition here.

_____

_____

_____

WORD LIST
forum
resolve
✔ delegate
humanitarian
✔ codify
justice
protest
dignity
negotiation
tribunal

Use Context Clues You have been introduced to two vocabulary words from the Eleanor Roosevelt article. Those words are checked off in the Word List here. In the first column below, write the other eight words from the Word List. In the second column, predict a meaning for each word. Then look up each word in your Word Wisdom Dictionary, and write the dictionary meaning that fits the context in the third column.

Vocabulary Word	Your Prediction	Dictionary Says
1		
2		
3		
4		
5		
6		
7		
8		

Process the Meanings

WORD LIST

forum

resolve

delegate

humanitarian

codify

justice

protest

dignity

negotiation

tribunal

Find the Antonyms Write the word from the Word List that means the opposite or nearly the opposite of each word or phrase below.

1 self-centered _____

2 agreement _____

3 stir up _____

4 shame _____

5 unfairness _____

Use Words Correctly in Writing Rewrite each sentence. Include the word in parentheses in your sentence.

6 The opposing groups needed a place to meet and discuss their differences. (forum)

_____

_____

7 Accused of a crime, the soldier faced the judges in the military court. (tribunal)

_____

8 The school committee will set down the rules that apply to all students. (codify)

_____

9 The realtors met with their clients to discuss their differences. (negotiations)

_____

10 Each nation sent someone to the trade meeting who would speak for its government's policies. (delegate)

_____

Apply What You've Learned

Complete the Analogies Choose the word that best completes each statement. Write your answer on the line.

1 Greedy is to selfish as **humanitarian** is to _____.
  a. kind   b. cruel   c. intelligent   d. guilty

2 Parent is to family as **delegate** is to _____.
  a. individual   b. committee   c. representative   d. meeting

3 Answer is to riddle as **resolve** is to _____.
  a. guess   b. test   c. problem   d. rule

4 Argument is to quarrel as **negotiation** is to _____.
  a. discussion   b. debate   c. solution   d. dispute

5 School is to principal as **tribunal** is to _____.
  a. party   b. child   c. family   d. judge

Complete the Statements Complete each statement by giving a good reason.

6 The voters attended the candidates' **forum** because _____

_____

7 Mr. Davio is demanding **justice** because _____

_____

8 Americans are allowed to hold **protests** because _____

_____

9 It is good that traffic laws are **codified** because _____

_____

10 When I am treated with **dignity**, I am pleased because _____

_____.

Write It! Write a dialogue between two people who disagree. Use Part 1 vocabulary words.

PART **2**

Latin Roots

for Word Wisdom

The Scopes Trial:

Law and Science

In 1925, a teacher named John Scopes was arrested. He had taught the theory of evolution to his students. At this time, teaching evolution was against the law in Tennessee. His trial is one of the most famous in American history.

The Book of Genesis tells the story of creation. Scientist Charles Darwin explained the concept of evolution. Some insist that evolution is scientific fact. Others do not believe that. This disagreement is not necessarily based on **prejudice**. It is often thought of as an argument between science and religion. In Dayton, Tennessee, these two explanations of human history clashed.

John Scopes, a science teacher, was teaching evolution to his high school students. The Butler Law made it **illegal** to teach evolution in Tennessee. This law had been passed a few months earlier. Some townspeople knew that they had a **legitimate** reason to take Scopes to court. Scopes was put on trial, and this new law was tested in the **judicial** system.

A man named William Jennings Bryan was part of the prosecution. He had run for president three times and was well known for his strong religious beliefs. On Scopes's defense team was Clarence Darrow. Darrow was another well-known man. He often questioned religious thinking. The stage was set for quite a courtroom battle.

Bryan had some of Scopes's high school students **testify** in court. He asked them to **attest** to the fact that Scopes had taught evolution. They described their teacher's lessons on evolution. Their witness **testimony** alone was enough to have Scopes found guilty. It was clear he had broken the Butler Law.

But Clarence Darrow had a different goal. He did not plan to prove that Scopes was innocent. He did not plan to **justify** Scopes's actions in the classroom. He wanted to show that the Butler Law was unfair. He planned to take the case to the Supreme Court. He hoped a higher court would **legalize** the teaching of the theory of evolution.

To the surprise of many, Darrow asked the jury to find Scopes guilty! As requested, the jury gave a guilty **judgment**. Scopes had to pay a one-hundred-dollar fine. A year later, the Tennessee Supreme Court changed the decision. But it didn't change everyone's mind. Today, the topic of evolution still causes quite a debate.

Practice the Context Clues Strategy Here is one of the boldfaced words from the essay on page 166. Use the context clues strategy you learned in Part 1 on page 161 to figure out the meaning of this word.

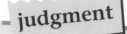

judgment

Read the sentence that uses the word *judgment*. Read some of the sentences around the word.

Look for context clues to the word's meaning. What **Words That Mean the Same** can you find?

_____

_____

_____

Think about the context clues. What other helpful information do you know?

_____

_____

_____

Predict a meaning for the word *judgment*.

_____

_____

_____

Check your Word Wisdom Dictionary to be sure of the meaning of the word *judgment*. Which of the meanings for *judgment* fits the context?

_____

_____

_____

Unlock the Meanings

In this unit you will study three new Latin roots that are related to the topic of legal matters. After you write the words from the Word List below, see if you can figure out how all the words with the same root are similar in meaning.

Latin Root: **jud, jur, jus**
meaning: law; right
English word: *justice*
meaning: fair treatment according to the law

Latin Root: **leg**
meaning: law; ambassador
English word: *delegate*
meaning: an official representative

Latin Root: **test**
meaning: witness
English word: *protest*
meaning: an objection

WORD LIST

- prejudice
- illegal
- legitimate
- judicial
- testify
- attest
- testimony
- justify
- legalize
- judgment

Sort by Roots Find the roots you just learned in the words in the Word List. Then write each word under the correct root. Think of other words you know that come from the same Latin root. Write each one in the correct place.

Legal Matters

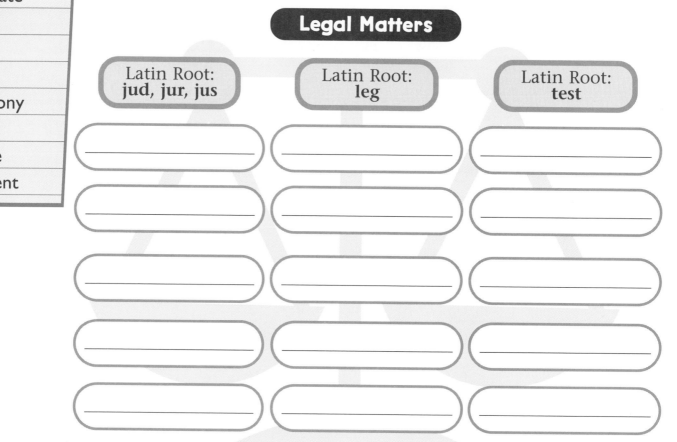

Latin Root: jud, jur, jus	Latin Root: leg	Latin Root: test

Prefix	Meaning
at-	to
il-	not

Example

at- (to) + **test** (witness) = **attest**

Use Roots and Prefixes Circle the root and any prefix you find in each boldfaced word. Then use context clues, roots, and prefixes to write the meaning of each word. Check your definitions in a dictionary.

1 Since I was at the beach too, I could **attest** that Kona was there.

_____

2 In my **judgment**, the hiking trail on the east side of the park is best.

_____

3 Senators debated whether or not to **legalize** some types of gambling.

_____

4 The **testimony** of a witness convinced the judge of the boy's guilt.

_____

5 Kate's winning record **justified** the coach's decision to let her pitch.

_____

6 The **judicial** branch of government is made up of different courts.

_____

7 Because Mrs. Shaw made an **illegal** turn, the officer gave her a ticket.

_____

8 Our laws must be fair and not show **prejudice** toward anyone.

_____

9 Mr. Lin **testified** in court that the company's files were destroyed.

_____

10 Brett is not the **legitimate** owner of the watch he found in the gym.

_____

Process the Meanings

WORD LIST

- prejudice
- illegal
- legitimate
- judicial
- testify
- attest
- testimony
- justify
- legalize
- judgment

Complete the Meanings Circle the letter of the item that best completes the sentence and explains the meaning of the boldfaced word.

1 A **legitimate** driver's license is one that is _____.
a. valid   b. brand new   c. a fake

2 If a man has a **prejudice**, he has an opinion that is _____.
a. common   b. unfair   c. foolish

3 Something that is **illegal** is not _____.
a. safe   b. healthy   c. permitted

4 When a person's actions are **justified**, they are thought to be _____.
a. helpful   b. unkind   c. fair or correct

5 A **testimony** is a statement of what a witness claims _____.
a. sounds best   b. is true   c. will please the jury

Choose the Correct Word Write the correct word from the Word List to complete each sentence.

6 Ella will be the first witness to _____ in the trial that begins today.

7 Tomas used good _____ when he decided to wear his seatbelt.

8 Since the water is now clean, the city will _____ swimming in Star Pond.

9 The president makes _____ appointments to the Supreme Court.

10 Because I saw the car crash, I could _____ to what happened.

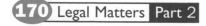

Apply What You've Learned

Complete the Analogies Choose the word that best completes each statement. Write the letter for your answer.

1 Presidential is to president as **judicial** is to _____.
   a. jury   b. judge   c. lawyer   d. courtroom

2 Kind is to thoughtful as **legitimate** is to _____.
   a. valid   b. unusual   c. false   d. careful

3 Stingy is to generous as **illegal** is to _____.
   a. different   b. unfair   c. lawful   d. attractive

4 Skill is to talent as **prejudice** is to _____.
   a. approval   b. unfairness   c. love   d. honesty

5 Argument is to lawyer as **testimony** is to _____.
   a. audience   b. officer   c. parent   d. witness

Complete the Sentences Complete each sentence.

6 If Dad asks about my schoolwork, my teacher can **attest** that

_____

7 Some people in our town want to **legalize** _____

_____

8 After stating her name, the witness **testified** that _____

_____

9 At camp, Maxine showed good **judgment** by _____

_____

10 Jamal felt **justified** in asking for a new computer because

_____

Speak It! Pretend you are a lawyer. Give a speech to convince a jury that your client is innocent. Use several Part 2 words.

PART 3 Reference Skills

for Word Wisdom

America:
Land of the Free!

You have learned a lot about the birth of our country. Let's look closely at the meetings that formed our nation. Read this article to learn more about the Continental Congresses.

The first Continental **Congress** met on September 5, 1774. About fifty men gathered in Philadelphia, Pennsylvania. King George III ruled England. His government had just passed new laws for the colonies, which England still governed. These laws were unfair to the colonists. They called these laws the Intolerable Acts.

The brave men at this **assembly** worked together to write a letter to King George. Writing this letter was an organized effort, or **campaign,** to get the king to change the new laws. But the king refused to do so.

The Second Continental Congress met on May 10, 1775. By this time, the American Revolution to free the colonies from British rule had begun. Most of the colonists wanted to establish their own government. They looked at King George as a **tyrant**. They did not like his stubborn ways. And they felt that he only cared about England. They believed that he only wanted to make money by taxing the colonies.

This important second meeting had **representatives** from almost every colony. This group of men was forced to act as a **federal** government, but there was no one to lead it. The delegates asked George Washington to build an army. They asked him to lead the battle for freedom. It was their goal to win **liberty** from the rule of England.

The representatives at the Second Continental Congress made some important decisions. They did not want a king to run this country. They wanted the people to have a say in the government. So, they made our country a **democracy**. And they wrote the Declaration of Independence, which was adopted on July 4, 1776.

Later, our Constitution was written. **Amendments** called the Bill of Rights were added to the Constitution. But the Declaration of Independence stands as the first important American document. When you read it, you will feel **patriotic** pride in our country and in the men who built it. Without the Declaration of Independence, the United States of America would be a very different country.

Practice the Context Clues Strategy Here is one of the boldfaced words from the article on page 172. Use the context clues strategy you learned in Part 1 on page 161 to figure out the meaning of this word.

campaign

Read the sentence that uses the word *campaign*. Read some of the sentences around the word.

Look for context clues to the word's meaning. What **Words That Mean the Same** can you find?

_____

_____

_____

Think about the context clues. What other helpful information do you know?

_____

_____

_____

Predict a meaning for the word *campaign*.

_____

_____

_____

Check your Word Wisdom Dictionary to be sure of the meaning of the word *campaign*. Which of the meanings for *campaign* fits the context?

_____

_____

_____

Unlock the Meanings

Researching on the Internet If you are writing a report, an Internet search engine can help you locate Web sites that are about your topic. Once you select a search engine, type in precise words that name your topic. Using precise vocabulary will help you find the most useful sites.

For example, if you wanted to find out about the amendments to the Constitution, you can just type in **amendments U.S. Constitution**.

Another way to narrow your search is to put quotation marks around any words that must appear together in a certain order, such as **"President John F. Kennedy."**

Write Search Entries Write a search entry for each topic below. Remember to use precise vocabulary, leaving out any unnecessary words. Use quotation marks around terms that must appear together.

1 subjects covered in Patrick Henry's patriotic speeches

_____

2 representatives in the U.S. Congress from the state of Texas

_____

3 why and how Clara Barton began the American Red Cross

_____

4 why the American colonies declared their independence from England

_____

5 how Harriet Tubman helped slaves escape on the underground railroad

_____

Find the Meaning

1. Use context clues.
2. Look for a familiar root, prefix, or suffix.
3. If the context or a word part doesn't help, check the dictionary.

Define the Words Follow the steps above to write the meaning of each boldfaced word. Write 1, 2, or 3 to show which steps you used.

WORD LIST
Congress
assembly
campaign
tyrant
representative
federal
liberty
democracy
amendment
patriotic

1 "America the Beautiful" is an example of a **patriotic** song.

_____

2 An **amendment** to the Constitution made slavery illegal.

_____

3 In a **democracy**, the people influence their government.

_____

4 Free speech is a **liberty** guaranteed to United States citizens.

_____

5 The **federal** government makes laws that affect all 50 states.

_____

6 Our scout troop sent one **representative** to the meeting.

_____

7 The king was a **tyrant** who treated everyone unfairly.

_____

8 **Congress** might soon pass stronger gun laws.

_____

9 The coach organized a **campaign** to raise money for the team.

_____

10 Principal Rivera spoke to the **assembly** of parents.

_____

Process the Meanings

WORD LIST

Congress
assembly
campaign
tyrant
representative
federal
liberty
democracy
amendment
patriotic

True or False? Write **T** or **F** to tell whether each statement is True or False.

1 In a **democracy,** all people can be involved with their country's government. _____

2 **Congress** decides whether someone is guilty of a crime. _____

3 If a student reads a science book, she is being **patriotic.** _____

4 **Representatives** make up their own laws. _____

5 An **amendment** can be an addition to a legal document. _____

Choose the Correct Meaning Circle the letter of the item that gives the best meaning for the boldfaced word.

6 obeyed the **tyrant**
a. a wise leader
b. a cruel leader
c. an old leader

7 a political **campaign**
a. a difficult debate
b. a close election
c. a set of activities

8 an **assembly** of teachers
a. a gathering
b. a march
c. a disagreement

9 fought for **liberty**
a. power
b. freedom
c. a change

10 a **federal** tax
a. large
b. state
c. national

11 a meeting of **Congress**
a. followers
b. geniuses
c. ruling group

12 a **patriotic** idea
a. showing love of country
b. emotional
c. strong

13 an **amendment** to the law
a. a note
b. a change
c. a governing body

14 a state **representative**
a. a delegate
b. a friend
c. a president

15 one **democracy**
a. estate
b. debate
c. government by the people

Apply What You've Learned

Categorize the Words Write a word from the Word List to complete each group.

1 governor, senator, _____

2 freedom, independence, _____

3 ruler, master, dictator, _____

4 monarchy, dictatorship, _____

5 revision, modification, alteration, _____

6 president, Supreme Court, _____

Demonstrate Word Knowledge Use what you have learned about the boldfaced words to answer the questions.

7 How is a **federal** law different from a state law? _____

_____

8 If you wanted to show you are **patriotic**, what could you do?

_____

9 Where might you see an **assembly** of reporters? _____

_____

10 What are some activities that are usually part of an election **campaign**?

_____

Write It! Imagine that you are a television reporter covering an important election. Write your script for the evening news. Use as many words from the Part 3 Word List as possible.

Review
for Word Wisdom

WORD LIST

forum
resolve
delegate
humanitarian
codify
justice
protest
dignity
negotiation
tribunal
prejudice
illegal
legitimate
judicial
testify
attest
testimony
justify
legalize
judgment
Congress
assembly
campaign
tyrant
representative
federal
liberty
democracy
amendment
patriotic

Categorize the Words Choose vocabulary words to write in each section below. The number in each heading tells you how many words to list.

Words with the same Latin root as *contest* 4	Places in which people meet to discuss opinions and facts 4	Synonyms for elected officials who serve voters 2

Write a Paragraph Choose five words from the Word List that are not listed above. Write your own paragraph that shows you know the meaning of these five words.

Choose the Word Circle the best word in parentheses to complete each sentence.

1 It is wrong for a judge to show (prejudice; judicial).

2 We sang (patriotic; legitimate) songs on July Fourth.

3 Listen to the candidates' speeches during their political (delegates; campaigns).

4 People can vote in a (delegate; democracy).

5 The Red Cross and other (attested; humanitarian) organizations helped victims of the earthquake.

Rewrite Sentences Read each sentence. Then use both boldfaced words to rewrite the sentence without changing its meaning. You may add or change an ending in the words.

6 It is against the law to take away someone's freedom without a fair trial. **illegal, liberty**

_____

7 The harsh ruler had no concern for fairness. **justice, tyrant**

_____

8 The lawmakers will spell out the details of the law that allows more government spending. **codify, legalize**

_____

9 Ms. Barilla treated everyone with respect and performed many generous deeds. **humanitarian, dignity**

_____

10 The witnesses claimed they had told the truth to the judges in a court of law. **tribunal, testimony**

_____

Review

Taking Vocabulary Tests

TEST-TAKING STRATEGY

Reading tests may include vocabulary words for you to define. In these tests, you might be asked to read a passage in which a word is highlighted. Then a test item asks about the meaning of that word. Clues in the context will help you figure out the meaning of the word. Think about the context because the word may be used in a new way.

Sample:

Read the paragraph. Fill in the circle of the item that BEST completes the statement.

The U.S. Constitution is 1
called a living document. 2
Americans are always 3
debating what that means. 4
Our Constitution is as *vital* 5
today as when it was written 6
more than 200 years ago. 7

In line 5, **vital** is best defined as

Ⓐ necessary
Ⓑ debatable
Ⓒ wonderful
Ⓓ nutritious

Practice Test   Read each paragraph. Fill in the circle of the item that BEST completes the statement.

1   The Declaration of Independence was adopted 1
in 1776. The American colonists had spent years 2
trying to persuade the British government to 3
treat them more fairly. Then Americans decided 4
that there would be no further *negotiations* with 5
Great Britain. 6

In line 5, the word **negotiations** is best defined as

Ⓐ disputes   Ⓒ trade
Ⓑ documents   Ⓓ discussions

2   The signers of the Declaration of Independence 1
knew they were committing treason against their 2
own government, Great Britain. Treason was a 3
crime punishable by death. Yet these Americans 4
believed strongly in their *legitimate* cause. 5

In line 5, the word **legitimate** is best defined as

Ⓐ valid   Ⓒ valuable
Ⓑ criminal   Ⓓ sensible

3   The country's Founders hoped that future 1
Americans would be extremely careful about 2
changing the Constitution. The document itself 3
explains the steps lawmakers must take to make 4
an *amendment* to the U.S. Constitution. 5

In line 5, **amendment** is best defined as

Ⓐ a law   Ⓒ a new idea
Ⓑ a formal change Ⓓ an improvement

4   The U.S. has two major political parties, the 1
Democrats and the Republicans. When the 2
nation was founded, there were no political 3
parties. George Washington, the first president, 4
hoped to *resolve* disagreements without political 5
competition. 6

In line 5, the word **resolve** is best defined as

Ⓐ to fix again   Ⓒ to agree
Ⓑ to be firm that Ⓓ to solve

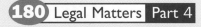

Play with Language

Hink Pinks A Hink Pink is a pair of one-syllable rhyming words that are the answer to a riddle. Here's an example:

What do you call a picture of valentines? *heart art*

Vocabulary words are boldfaced in each riddle below. Use what you know to write the Hink Pink that answers the riddle. The first letter of each word is given as a hint.

1 What do you call a person who makes the **judicial** decision about a prize-winning candy? a f_____

j_____

2 What do you call a favorite among the fifty in our **federal** union? a g_____ s_____

3 What do you call a **justified** demand to perform a brave act?

a f_____ d_____

4 What do you call a **tyrant's** harsh reign?

a c_____ r_____

5 What might someone say to **protest** soft white crystals of ice?

n_____ s_____

Speak It! The Declaration of Independence includes a famous statement that begins, "We hold these truths to be self-evident ...." The United States Constitution begins with a famous Preamble. Choose one of the documents, read the famous passage, and memorize it. Then recite it to your class.

PART 1

Context Clues

for Word Wisdom

Woman Overboard!

Adventure stories can be amazing, especially when they are true. Read this inspiring true story of adventure and survival.

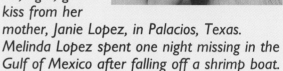

Melinda Lopez, 32, right, gets a kiss from her mother, Janie Lopez, in Palacios, Texas. Melinda Lopez spent one night missing in the Gulf of Mexico after falling off a shrimp boat.

PHOTO: © HOUSTON CHRONICLE

Good and Bad

UNIT 9

Late afternoon, Tuesday, October 7, 2003, Melinda Lopez was taking a break from her work on a shrimp boat in the Gulf of Mexico. She began climbing to a comfortable place to read. Suddenly, her shoe came off, and she slipped. She tumbled off the boat.

She watched, **aghast**, as the boat continued on its way. Alone in the cold, choppy water, she had no life vest, only a shirt and shorts.

Lopez began swimming. She was a capable swimmer, but the coast was seventy miles away!

In the darkness, Lopez swam and floated alone in the black, **featureless** water. Would sharks or poisonous jellyfish attack her? She tried not to let her fear be a **distraction** from her one goal—survival. Something large bumped her. She knocked it away. It then bumped her again, hard. Finally, it was gone.

After what seemed an **eternity**, Lopez heard a bell ringing. The sound came from an offshore oil platform. She battled the **arduous**

current to get to the platform's ladder and pulled herself up. Unfortunately, the oil rig was **abandoned**.

She had been in the water for thirteen **hazardous** hours! Shivering and suffering from extreme **fatigue**, Lopez fought against confusion. Her eyes were swollen from the salt water, but she searched the rig. She discovered a can of spray paint and climbed to the helicopter landing pad. There, she painted a large SOS. She found discarded water bottles and drank what little water was left in them. The morning and afternoon passed. The thought of another cold night was **agony**. Then, about 6:30 P.M., Lopez heard a helicopter overhead. The Coast Guard had spotted her SOS sign!

Melinda Lopez was taken to a Texas hospital, where she quickly recovered from her **ordeal**. Reporters wanted to know how she had managed to survive. "I just had to stay strong," she explained.

Context Clues Strategy

Look for the Location or Setting

EXAMPLE: The dam burst, and the freed water roared downstream. Uprooted trees spun and crashed in the *turbulent* water.

CLUE: The words *roared downstream* and *trees spun and crashed* help you picture the water in this setting. You can guess that *turbulent* water is fast and dangerous.

Here are the steps for using this context clues strategy to figure out the meaning of the word *aghast* from the article on page 182.

Read the sentence with the unknown word and some of the sentences around it.

*She watched, **aghast**, as the boat continued on its way. Alone in the cold, choppy water, she had no life vest, only a shirt and shorts.*

Look for context clues. What words can you find about the **Location or Setting?**

The words *cold, choppy water* describe the location.

Think about the context clues and other information you may already know.

Being alone without a life vest in cold water and seeing the boat disappear sounds terrifying.

Predict a meaning for the word.

The word *aghast* must mean "terrified."

Check the Word Wisdom Dictionary to be sure of the meaning.

The word *aghast* means "terrified or shocked."

Unlock the Meanings

Practice the Strategy Here is one of the boldfaced words from the article on page 182. Use the context clues strategy on page 183 to figure out the meaning of the word.

featureless

Read the sentence that includes the word *featureless* and some of the sentences around it.

Look for context clues to the word's meaning. What words can you find about the **Location or Setting?**

_____

_____

_____

Think about the context clues. What other helpful information do you know?

_____

_____

_____

Predict a meaning for the word *featureless*.

_____

_____

_____

Check the Word Wisdom Dictionary to be sure of the meaning of *featureless*. Write the definition here.

_____

_____

Use Context Clues You have been introduced to two vocabulary words from the article on page 182. Those words are checked off in the Word List. In the first column below, write the other eight words from the Word List. Use context clues to predict a meaning for each word in the second column. Then look up the meanings in the Word Wisdom Dictionary. Write the definition in the third column.

WORD LIST

✔aghast
✔featureless
distraction
eternity
arduous
abandon
hazardous
fatigue
agony
ordeal

Vocabulary Word	Your Prediction	Dictionary Says
1		
2		
3		
4		
5		
6		
7		
8		

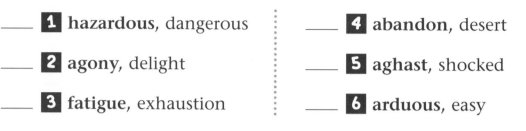

Process the Meanings

WORD LIST

- aghast
- featureless
- distraction
- eternity
- arduous
- abandon
- hazardous
- fatigue
- agony
- ordeal

Identify Synonyms and Antonyms Read each pair of words. Write **S** if the words are synonyms. Write **A** if the words are antonyms.

_____ **1** **hazardous**, dangerous

_____ **2** **agony**, delight

_____ **3** **fatigue**, exhaustion

_____ **4** **abandon**, desert

_____ **5** **aghast**, shocked

_____ **6** **arduous**, easy

Use the Words Correctly in Writing Rewrite each sentence. Include the word from the Word List in parentheses in your sentence.

7 The flat landscape seemed the same in all directions. (featureless)

_____

_____

8 The gymnast did not pay any attention to the noise of the crowd. (distraction)

_____

_____

9 The week seemed endless, but at last Pamela's birthday arrived. (eternity)

_____

_____

10 For the Phan family, reaching the United States was a test of survival. (ordeal)

_____

_____

Apply What You've Learned

Use the Words Correctly in Writing Read the boldfaced words below. Use each word correctly in a sentence.

1 hazardous _____

2 featureless _____

3 arduous _____

4 aghast _____

5 eternity _____

Demonstrate Word Knowledge Answer the questions.

6 How can you reduce **distractions** when you're doing homework?

_____

7 What are two things that might cause you to feel **fatigue**?

_____

8 How would you feel if you were told to prepare for an **ordeal**?

_____

9 If your friend is in **agony**, how can you tell?

_____

10 Why might sailors **abandon** their ship?

_____

Write It! Write an adventure story with danger and suspense. Use as many vocabulary words from Part 1 as you can.

PART 2

Latin and Greek Roots

for Word Wisdom

Ahoy, Matey!

All About Pirates

Do you believe that pirates were real? Or are they just legends? Well, in reality, they are a little of both.

When you think of the pirates Blackbeard, Long John Silver, Captain Hook, and William Kidd, you probably think of storybooks and movies. But many well-known pirates were real.

Blackbeard and William Kidd are examples of **bona fide** pirates. However, some pirates, like Long John Silver, were just storybook characters—Long John was made up by Robert Louis Stevenson and is the **antagonist** in the novel *Treasure Island*. Long John Silver is the rival of Jim Hawkins, the **protagonist,** or main character, of the novel.

Pirates had bad reputations. They were well known for their **maltreatment** of people. They were most interested in finding a **bonanza** of gold and other treasures on board ships. They attacked large ships and then **antagonized** the passengers by teasing them and threatening them with weapons. They some-times forced the passengers off the ships and onto lifeboats. Sometimes they would steal the ship, too. If a pirate stole all of your money and your boat, you would be an out-spoken **detractor** of pirates!

Some governments would hire sailors to rid the seas of pirates. These sailors were offered a large **bounty** for the capture of certain pirates. Blackbeard was the first name on a list of most-wanted pirates. His real name was Edward Teach, and some experts think he was born in England. One thing is for sure: Blackbeard was the most-feared pirate of his day. Even his crew was afraid of him!

However, a man named Robert Maynard was not afraid of Black-beard. In the fall of 1718, Maynard and his crew attacked Blackbeard's ship. The battle was definitely not **protracted**. Within a short time, Blackbeard was dead. As an added **bonus,** Maynard kept Blackbeard's ship. People even say that Maynard sailed away with Blackbeard's head on a pole!

It seems that pirate stories are a combination of fact and fiction. But even the legends are based on some facts.

Practice the Context Clues Strategy   Here is one of the boldfaced words from the essay on page 188. Use the context clues strategy you learned in Part 1 on page 183 to figure out the meaning of this word.

bonanza

📖 **Read** the sentence that uses the word *bonanza*. Read some of the sentences around the word.

🔍 **Look** for context clues to the word's meaning. What words about the **Location or Setting** can you find?

_____

_____

_____

💡 **Think** about the context clues. What other helpful information do you know?

_____

_____

_____

➡️ **Predict** a meaning for the word *bonanza*.

_____

_____

_____

✔️ **Check** your Word Wisdom Dictionary to be sure of the meaning of the word *bonanza*. Write the definition here.

_____

_____

_____

Unlock the Meanings

You know that many English words have a Latin or a Greek root. The roots you will study in this unit all have to do with the topic of good and bad things. Knowing the meanings of these roots will help you understand the meanings of many new words.

Greek Root: **agon**
meaning: struggle
English word: *agony*
meaning: great pain or suffering

Latin Root: **bon, boun**
meaning: good
English word: *bonbon*
meaning: a piece of candy

Latin Root: **tract, treat**
meaning: to drag, to pull, or to draw
English word: *distraction*
meaning: something that draws away attention

WORD LIST

bona fide
antagonist
protagonist
maltreatment
bonanza
antagonize
detractor
bounty
protract
bonus

Sort by Roots Find the roots you just learned in the Word List. Then write each word in the correct column. Think of other words you know that come from the same Latin or Greek root. Write each one in the correct column.

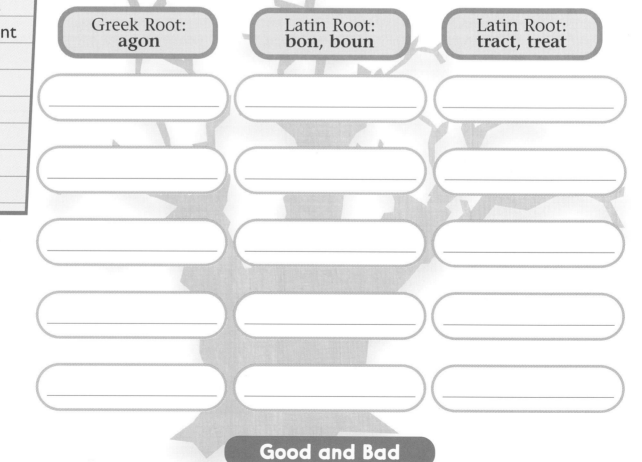

Greek Root: **agon**	Latin Root: **bon, boun**	Latin Root: **tract, treat**

Good and Bad

Prefix	Meaning
mal-	bad
de-	away, down

Example

mal- (bad) + **treat** (draw) + **-ment** (noun) = **maltreatment**

Use Roots and Prefixes Circle the root and any prefix you find in each boldfaced word. Then use context clues, roots, and prefixes to write the meaning of each word. Check your definitions in the Word Wisdom Dictionary.

1 Laws in the United States protect workers from **maltreatment**.

_____

2 The **bounty** of the charities helped the people who lost their homes.

_____

3 Colin's practical jokes sometimes **antagonized** even his best friends.

_____

4 Our mayor's most outspoken **detractor** often criticizes her decisions.

_____

5 Winning the high jump made Fia happy. Receiving a trophy was a **bonus**!

_____

6 The **protagonist** had more lines than anyone else in our school play.

_____

7 Finding the lost treasure was a **bonanza** for the expedition.

_____

8 When their countries were at war, the two generals were **antagonists**.

_____

9 The canceled return flight forced me to **protract** my trip to Italy.

_____

10 The divers discovered a **bona fide** pirate ship at the bottom of the ocean.

_____

Process the Meanings

WORD LIST

- bona fide
- antagonist
- protagonist
- maltreatment
- bonanza
- antagonize
- detractor
- bounty
- protract
- bonus

Write Synonyms Write a word from the Word List that is a synonym for each underlined word.

1 the <u>abuse</u> of animals _____

2 a determined <u>opponent</u> _____

3 one <u>genuine</u> Civil War uniform _____

4 the <u>generosity</u> of the community _____

5 will <u>lengthen</u> the wait _____

6 might <u>anger</u> some neighbors _____

Revise Sentences Rewrite each sentence. Replace the underlined words with a word from the Word List.

7 In my favorite mystery, the <u>main character</u> tries to find a missing suitcase.

_____

_____

8 Each clerk received a <u>special, unexpected reward</u> of six extra vacation days.

_____

9 The author ignored the remarks of the <u>person who disliked his book</u>.

_____

10 European explorers hoped their discoveries would be a <u>source of great wealth</u>.

_____

_____

Apply What You've Learned

Complete the Analogies Choose the word that best completes each analogy. Write your answer on the line.

1 Villain is to hero as **detractor** is to _____.

    a. teammate   b. comrade   c. supporter   d. complainer

2 Exercise is to jogging as **maltreatment** is to _____.

    a. hitting   b. smiling   c. hugging   d. running

3 Helpful is to harmful as **bona fide** is to _____.

    a. real   b. fake   c. genuine   d. sincere

4 Sweetheart is to darling as **antagonist** is to _____.

    a. friend   b. ruler   c. boss   d. enemy

5 Drummer is to musician as **protagonist** is to _____.

    a. person   b. character   c. play   d. hero

6 Happy is to sad as **bonanza** is to _____.

    a. money   b. wealth   c. poverty   d. loss

Give Examples Write an example for each description below.

7 a way that someone might **antagonize** you _____

_____

8 a time when the **bounty** of your family helped someone _____

_____

9 an event that led to a **protracted** ride home or to another destination

_____

10 a time when you received an unexpected **bonus** _____

_____

Speak It! Talk about some good things you have seen lately. Use several Part 2 vocabulary words.

PART 3 Reference Skills

for Word Wisdom

A Greek Myth:
The Story of Odysseus

Greek mythology is full of exciting, adventurous stories. Read this article to learn more about Odysseus.

Homer was a poet in ancient Greece. He is especially famous for two long story-poems: *The Iliad* and *The Odyssey*. These are both **superb** accounts of Greek myths. *The Iliad* tells the story of Achilles during the Trojan War. It is one of the earliest books about Greek myths.

You can think of *The Odyssey* as the sequel, or follow-up, to *The Iliad*. The main character of *The Odyssey* is Odysseus. He is a Greek soldier who fought in the Trojan War. *The Odyssey* tells the story of what happened to Odysseus after the war.

The gods Athena and Poseidon were both angry with the Greeks. After the war, the Greeks did not thank the gods like they should have. Athena and Poseidon were both **vindictive** gods. They wanted revenge. They decided to teach the Greeks a lesson.

Poseidon was the god of the sea. As the Greeks sailed their ships back to Greece after the war, he created a **brutal** storm that shipwrecked most of the Greek fleet.

Many men drowned, but Odysseus did not.

Odysseus wandered, lost at sea, for years. Then, he was trapped on an island for a long time. Finally, the gods forgave Odysseus and wanted to help him get back home to his family. Odysseus took this **opportunity** and set sail from the island. Poseidon did not make this voyage **convenient** for him— Poseidon was still angry. Odysseus faced many storms before finally reaching his homeland.

Once home, Odysseus found many strange men in his house. They were trying to convince his wife, Penelope, to forget about Odysseus and marry one of them. Penelope had many **virtues,** including faithfulness to her husband. Odysseus would not let these men **humiliate** him in his own house. He would take revenge. This time, he would have one great **advantage**: The goddess Athena would help him.

Odysseus **deceived** everyone in his house. He sneaked in disguised as an old man. He found all the strange men, and then **chaos** broke out in the house. Odysseus won a huge battle. After that, he became a part of his family again.

Practice the Context Clues Strategy   Here is one of the boldfaced words from the essay on page 194. Use the context clues strategy you learned in Part 1 on page 183 to figure out the meaning of this word.

humiliate

 Read the sentence that uses the word *humiliate*. Read some of the sentences around the word.

 Look for context clues to the word's meaning. What words about the **Location or Setting** can you find?

_____

_____

_____

Think about the context clues. What other helpful information do you know?

_____

_____

 Predict a meaning for the word *humiliate*.

_____

_____

_____

Check your Word Wisdom Dictionary to be sure of the meaning of the word *humiliate*. Write the definition here.

_____

_____

_____

Unlock the Meanings

Choosing the Right Reference When you need information to write a report or another kind of paper, where should you look?

Use a **dictionary** if you want to find
- how to spell a word, pronounce a word, or divide it into syllables
- a word's part of speech
- what a word means
- different forms of a word
- a word's history

Use a **thesaurus** if you want to find
- synonyms for a word
- antonyms for a word

Use an **encyclopedia** if you want to find
- factual articles about people, places, things, and events
- charts, graphs, diagrams, maps, and photographs on a variety of topics

Identify References Write **dictionary, thesaurus,** or **encyclopedia** to tell where you would find each item below.

1 the correct pronunciation of *vindictive* _____

2 a list of synonyms for *superb* _____

3 antonyms for *advantage* _____

4 the parts of speech for *humiliate* and *humiliation* _____

5 a more exact word for *easy* _____

6 a history of the Olympics _____

7 a map of Greece _____

8 a sample sentence that includes *virtue* _____

9 a synonym for *brutal* _____

10 the history of the word *chaos* _____

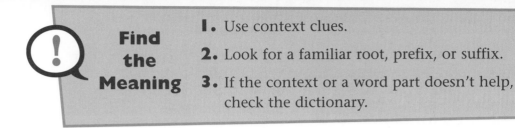

Find the Meaning

1. Use context clues.
2. Look for a familiar root, prefix, or suffix.
3. If the context or a word part doesn't help, check the dictionary.

WORD LIST

superb

vindictive

brutal

opportunity

convenient

virtue

humiliate

advantage

deceive

chaos

Define the Words Follow the steps to write the meaning of each boldfaced word. Write 1, 2, or 3 to show which steps you used.

1 The mall is a **convenient** place to shop.

_____

2 I won three tickets, so we had an **opportunity** to go to the circus.

_____

3 Politicians sometimes **deceive** when they make promises.

_____

4 The trash added to the **chaos** in the house after the party.

_____

5 Long fingers are an **advantage** for learning to play the piano.

_____

6 My teacher has many **virtues**, including kindness and patience.

_____

7 Ten people were seriously injured during the **brutal** attack.

_____

8 Losing by twelve runs **humiliated** the coach and team.

_____

9 The **vindictive** man took the driver who hit his car to court.

_____

10 A clear sky and a steady wind made it a **superb** day for kite flying.

_____

WORD LIST

- superb
- vindictive
- brutal
- opportunity
- convenient
- virtue
- humiliate
- advantage
- deceive
- chaos

Write Antonyms Write a word from the Word List that is an antonym for each underlined word.

1 her <u>poor</u> performance _____

2 a <u>forgiving</u> person _____

3 one <u>drawback</u> of the plan _____

4 will <u>praise</u> the winner _____

5 the <u>calm</u> after the alarm rang _____

Answer True or False Write **T** or **F** to tell whether each statement is true or false. Write a sentence to explain your answer.

6 Shoppers can be **deceived** by false advertising. _____

_____

7 Laziness is usually thought of as a **virtue**. _____

_____

8 A **convenient** kitchen appliance is hard to use. _____

_____

9 An **opportunity** gives you the chance to do something desirable. _____

_____

10 Someone who treats people in a **brutal** way is considered kind. _____

_____

Apply What You've Learned

Find Examples Read each description. Then put a check beside every example that matches the description.

1 times when someone might feel **humiliated**

____ getting caught stealing   ____ getting a good grade

2 ways in which a sports team can have an **advantage** over other teams

____ having great players   ____ wearing fancy uniforms

3 events that often result in **chaos**

____ an explosion   ____ a cloudy day

4 actions that are meant to **deceive** someone

____ wearing a new shirt   ____ saying something that isn't true

5 qualities that are considered **virtues**

____ shyness   ____ generosity

6 things that might be described as **brutal**

____ a broken bicycle   ____ a battle

Give Reasons Write **yes** or **no** to answer each question. Then write a sentence that explains your reason(s).

7 Would a chance to fly on the space shuttle be a good **opportunity**?

_____

8 Would you behave in a **vindictive** way if you were punched?

_____

9 Are handheld computers **convenient** for sending e-mail?

_____

10 Would a well-prepared meal be **superb**?

_____

Write It! Write a description of a character from a book. Use several Part 3 vocabulary words.

Review

for Word Wisdom

WORD LIST

- aghast
- featureless
- distraction
- eternity
- arduous
- abandon
- hazardous
- fatigue
- agony
- ordeal
- bona fide
- antagonist
- protagonist
- maltreatment
- bonanza
- antagonize
- detractor
- bounty
- protract
- bonus
- superb
- vindictive
- brutal
- opportunity
- convenient
- virtue
- humiliate
- advantage
- deceive
- chaos

Sort by Part of Speech and Meaning Choose vocabulary words to write in each section below. Not every word will fit in one of the four sections.

Nouns that name things people may enjoy or approve of	Adjectives that describe good things	Adjectives that describe disliked or hated things	Verbs that show what mean-spirited people may do

Choose the Correct Words Write the word from
the Word List that best completes each sentence.

1 In an adventure story, the _____ faces danger

and takes risks.

2 The American Society for the Prevention of Cruelty to Animals

tries to stop the _____ of animals.

3 Dabney muttered this _____ threat: "I'll get

even with you someday!"

4 My brother is four inches taller than I am, so he has a definite

_____ when we play basketball.

5 I hope that Mel is telling the truth and not trying to

_____ anyone.

6 If you ever have the _____ to travel to

another country, take it!

7 Everyone was _____ at the shocking news.

8 Each camp counselor received a(n) _____ of

$100 at the end of the summer.

9 After a month, the shipwrecked sailors were rescued, and their

_____ended.

10 Somehow, the sculptor turned the _____

lump of clay into an expressive face.

Taking Vocabulary Tests

Taking tests is a skill that can improve with practice. Always review a test after it has been corrected. Look at any errors you made. Think and talk about why you made them. You may be able to avoid similar errors on future tests.

On tests of antonyms, remember that you are looking for a word with an opposite meaning. A word with a similar meaning, or synonym, is often among the answer choices. Stay focused on what you are asked to do.

Sample:

Fill in the letter of the item that most nearly means the OPPOSITE of the underlined word.

a <u>useful</u> tool

(A) worthless
(B) handy
(C) helpful
(D) dangerous

Practice Test Fill in the letter of the item that most nearly means the OPPOSITE of the underlined vocabulary word.

1 a remark that <u>humiliates</u>
(A) amuses
(B) embarrasses
(C) shames
(D) honors

2 <u>hazardous</u> materials
(A) poisonous
(B) safe
(C) dangerous
(D) wet

3 an <u>abandoned</u> building
(A) occupied
(B) old
(C) repaired
(D) tall

4 a <u>protracted</u> delay
(A) prolonged
(B) preventable
(C) short
(D) time-consuming

5 a <u>bona fide</u> coin
(A) fake
(B) valuable
(C) real
(D) ancient

6 the <u>arduous</u> journey
(A) hard
(B) comfortable
(C) long
(D) unnecessary

7 the <u>superb</u> meal
(A) breakfast
(B) morning
(C) excellent
(D) disgusting

8 comments from the <u>detractor</u>
(A) attractive person
(B) reviewer
(C) supporter
(D) thinker

9 a feeling of <u>fatigue</u>
(A) energy
(B) weariness
(C) worry
(D) horror

10 the hero's <u>antagonist</u>
(A) enemy
(B) friend
(C) protagonist
(D) adventure

Build New Words

Find and Use Suffixes Look again at the Word List on page 200. Find the words that have these suffixes: *-ize, -ion, -ity, -or, -ous*. List them in the correct box below.

-ize	-ion	-ity	-or	-ous
_____	_____	_____	_____	_____
		_____		_____

Add one of the five suffixes to each word in the chart below to make a real word. Write the suffix and the new word. Each word should match the listed meaning. You may need to check a dictionary.

Word	+ Suffix	= New Word	Meaning
agony			to struggle
protract			a device for drawing angles
bounty			generous
brutal			cruelty
brutal			to treat extremely harshly
humiliate			the condition of shame or disgrace
virtue			having high morals
advantage			improving the chance of success

Speak It! Think of several ways to complete each of these two sentences. Use vocabulary words from this unit.

It's good to _____. It's bad to _____.

Take turns reading the two sentences in small groups.

W!rd Wisdom Dictionary

PRONUNCIATION KEY

/ă/	pat
/ā/	pay
/â/	care
/ä/	father
/är/	far
/ĕ/	pet
/ē/	be
/ĭ/	pit
/ī/	pie
/îr/	pier
/ŏ/	mop
/ō/	toe
/ô/	paw, for
/oi/	noise
/ou/	out
/o͝o/	look
/o͞o/	boot
/ŭ/	cut
/ûr/	urge
/th/	thin
/*th*/	this
/hw/	what
/zh/	vision
/ə/	about
	item
	pencil
	gallop
	circus
/ər/	butter

A

a•ban•don /ə băn′ dən/ *v.* **a•ban•doned, a•ban•don•ing, a•ban•dons.** to leave behind; to give up. *The passengers abandoned the sinking ship.* —**a•ban•don•ment** *n.*

a•bun•dant /ə bŭn′ dənt/ *adj.* plentiful. *The squirrels have an abundant supply of acorns.* —**a•bun•dant•ly** *adv.*

ac•cel•er•ate[1] /ăk sĕl′ ə rāt′/ *v.* **ac•cel•er•at•ed, ac•cel•er•at•ing, ac•cel•er•ates.** to go faster. *The sled accelerates as it goes down the hill.* —**ac•cel•er•a•tive** *adj.* —**ac•cel•er•a•tion** *n.*

ac•cel•er•ate[2] /ăk sĕl′ ə rāt′/ *v.* **ac•cel•er•at•ed, ac•cel•er•at•ing, ac•cel•er•ates.** to make to go faster. *Moving the pedals faster will accelerate the bicycle.* —**ac•cel•er•a•tive** *adj.* —**ac•cel•er•a•tion** *n.*

ac•cen•tu•ate /ăk sĕn′ cho͞o āt′/ *v.* **ac•cen•tu•at•ed, ac•cen•tu•at•ing, ac•cen•tu•ates.** to make more noticeable; to emphasize; to stress. *Underlining a word accentuates it.* —**ac•cen•tu•a•tion** *n.*

ac•cess /ăk′ sĕs/ *n., pl.* **ac•cess•es.** a means of approaching, entering, exiting, or making use of. *The front door provided the only access to the store.*

ac•claim[1] /ə klām′/ *n.* praise; enthusiastic applause. *The actor received acclaim for his outstanding performance.*

ac•claim[2] /ə klām′/ *v.* **ac•claimed, ac•claim•ing, ac•claims.** to praise; to applaud. *Everyone acclaimed the football team for winning the championship.*

ac•com•plish /ə kŏm′ plĭsh/ *v.* **ac•com•plished, ac•com•plish•ing, ac•com•plish•es.** to succeed in doing; to perform. *I hope to accomplish my goal of getting good grades.*

ac•cu•mu•late /ə kyo͞om′ yə lāt′/ *v.* **ac•cu•mu•lat•ed, ac•cu•mu•lat•ing, ac•cu•mu•lates.** to collect little by little; to gather. *I have accumulated many books.*

ac•cu•mu•la•tion /ə kyo͞om′ yə lā′ shən/ *n.* the act of gathering or amassing, as into a heap. *The accumulation of snow forced the cancellation of school.*

ac•cu•rate /ăk′ yər ĭt/ *adj.* without errors; correct. *I made an accurate count of the pennies I have saved.* —**ac•cu•rate•ly** *adv.* —**ac•cu•rate•ness** *n.*

a•cous•tics /ə ko͞o′ stĭks/ *n.* the features of a room or space that determine how well sounds can be heard in it. *The acoustics in the new theater were wonderful.*

ac•ro•nym /ăk′ rə nĭm′/ *n.* a word formed from the first letters or syllables of other words. *NASA is the acronym for National Aeronautics and Space Administration.*

ac•ti•vate /ăk′ tə vāt′/ *v.* **ac•ti•vat•ed, ac•ti•vat•ing, ac•ti•vates.** to make active; to put in motion. *I pushed a number on the keypad to activate the alarm system.* —**ac•ti•va•tion** *n.* —**ac•ti•va•tor** *n.*

ad•min•is•tra•tor /ăd mĭn′ ĭ strā′ tər/ *n.* a person who manages or takes charge. *The nursing administrator met with the doctors.*

ad•van•tage /ăd văn′ tĭj/ *n.* a benefit; a favorable position. *Being first in line is an advantage to getting good seats at the play.*

ad•van•ta•geous /ăd′ văn tā′ jəs/ *adj.* beneficial. *The extra practice was advantageous.* —**ad•van•ta•geous•ly** *adv.* —**ad•van•ta•geous•ness** *n.*

af•flu•ent /ăf′ lōō ənt/ *adj.* wealthy; rich. *Our affluent neighbors own several vacation homes.* —**af•flu•ent•ly** *adv.*

a•ghast /ə găst′/ *adj.* terrified or shocked. *People were aghast when the building caught on fire.*

ag•ile /ăj′ əl *or* ăj′ īl′/ *adj.* able to move or think easily or quickly. *Our agile cat jumped on top of the refrigerator.* —**ag•ile•ly** *adv.* —**ag•ile•ness** *n.* —**a•gil•i•ty** *n.*

ag•i•tate /ăj′ ĭ tāt′/ *v.* **ag•i•tat•ed, ag•i•tat•ing, ag•i•tates.** to shake, move, or disturb roughly. *Strong winds agitated the trees.* —**ag•i•tat•ed•ly** *adv.*

ag•o•nize /ăg′ ə nīz′/ *v.* **ag•o•nized, ag•o•niz•ing, ag•o•niz•es.** to suffer extreme pain or great anguish. *I agonized from the pain of my broken arm.*

ag•o•ny /ăg′ ə nē/ *n., pl.* **ag•o•nies.** the suffering of severe pain. *Doctors tried to ease the patient's agony.*

al•lit•er•a•tion /ə lĭt′ ə rā′ shən/ *n.* the repetition of same beginning sounds in words. *The phrase "perfect peach punch" is an example of alliteration.*

am•a•teur¹ /ăm′ ə tûr′ *or* ăm′ ə tər′ *or* ăm′ ə chōōr′ *or* ăm′ ə chər *or* ăm′ ə tyōōr′/ *adj.* related to something done or performed for enjoyment rather than as a job or profession; not professional. *Many people enjoy amateur sports.* —**am•a•teur•ism** *n.*

am•a•teur² /ăm′ ə tûr′ *or* ăm′ ə tər′ *or* ăm′ ə chōōr′ *or* ăm′ ə chər *or* ăm′ ə tyōōr′/ *n.* a person who lacks skill or training. *The painting looked like it was done by an amateur.* —**am•a•teur•ism** *n.*

am•a•teur³ /ăm′ ə tûr′ *or* ăm′ ə tər′ *or* ăm′ ə chōōr′ *or* ăm′ ə chər *or* ăm′ ə tyōōr′/ *n.* a person who does something for enjoyment rather than as a profession. *Only amateurs can participate in the competition.* —**am•a•teur•ism** *n.*

a•mend•ment /ə mĕnd′ mənt/ *n.* a legal or formal change or addition to a law or group of laws. *The first ten amendments of the U.S. Constitution are called the Bill of Rights.*

a•nal•o•gy /ə năl′ ə jē/ *n., pl.* **a•nal•o•gies.** an explanation of something by comparing it to something else. *There is an analogy between the heart and a pump.*

a•non•y•mous /ə nŏn′ ə məs/ *adj.* nameless. *The anonymous caller did not leave a message.* —**a•non•y•mous•ly** *adv.*

an•tag•o•nist /ăn tăg′ ə nĭst/ *n.* a person who opposes, fights against, or competes with another. *The two politicians were natural antagonists.* —**an•tag•o•nis•tic** *adj.* —**an•tag•o•nis•ti•cal•ly** *adv.*

an•tag•o•nize /ăn tăg′ ə nīz′/ *v.* **an•tag•o•nized, an•tag•o•niz•ing, an•tag•o•niz•es.** to bring about a feeling of irritation or anger. *The phone's constant ringing antagonized us.*

ap•pa•ra•tus /ăp′ ə rā′ təs *or* ăp′ ə răt′ əs/ *n., pl.* **ap•pa•ra•tus** *or* **ap•pa•ra•tus•es.** a device or equipment used for a particular purpose; a machine. *A car jack is an apparatus that lifts a car so that a tire can be changed.*

ap•par•el /ə păr′ əl/ *n.* clothing. *I bought special apparel for the ski trip.*

ap•pe•tiz•er /ăp′ ĭ tī′ zər/ *n.* food or drink served before a meal to help increase the desire for food. *Before dinner our host served an appetizer of cheese and crackers.*

ap•pren•tice /ə prĕn' tĭs/ *n.* someone who is learning a job by working for an expert, often for little or no pay during the training period. *My older sister is an apprentice at a radio station.*

ap•ti•tude /ăp' tĭ to͞od' *or* ăp' tĭ tyo͞od'/ *n.* a talent or natural ability. *The young girl has an aptitude for playing the violin.*

ar•du•ous /är' jo͞o əs/ *adj.* requiring great effort; very difficult. *Training for a marathon is arduous work.* —**ar•du•ous•ly** *adv.* —**ar•du•ous•ness** *n.*

a•ro•ma /ə rō' mə/ *n.* a pleasant smell. *The aroma of roses filled the garden.*

as•sem•bly /ə sĕm' blē/ *n., pl.* **as•sem•blies.** a group of people gathered together for a common purpose. *The mayor gave a speech to an assembly of reporters.*

as•sert /ə sûrt'/ *v.* **as•sert•ed, as•sert•ing, as•serts.** to state positively; to declare to be true. *The witness asserted the cause of the accident with confidence.*

at•test¹ /ə tĕst'/ *v.* **at•test•ed, at•test•ing, at•tests.** to be a witness. *Dad can attest that I was studying last night.* —**at•test•ant** *n.*

at•test² /ə tĕst'/ *v.* **at•test•ed, at•test•ing, at•tests.** to be proof of or give evidence. *The melting snow attests the warmer temperature.* —**at•test•ant** *n.*

at•tract /ə trăkt'/ *v.* **at•tract•ed, at•tract•ing, at•tracts.** to pull or draw to or toward. *Soccer attracts many players because it has so much action.* —**at•tract•a•ble** *adj.* —**at•tract•er** *or* **at•trac•tor** *n.* —**at•trac•tion** *n.*

— Ⓑ —

bank•rupt /băngk' rŭpt' *or* băngk' rəpt/ *adj.* unable to pay one's bills. *The bankrupt company had to close all of its stores.*

bar•i•tone /băr' ĭ tōn'/ *n.* a male singer with a range lower than a tenor and higher than a bass. *The baritone's performance was outstanding.*

ben•e•fit¹ /bĕn' ə fĭt/ *n.* something that is helpful or makes a situation better. *A public swimming pool is one benefit to living in this neighborhood.*

ben•e•fit² /bĕn' ə fĭt/ *v.* **ben•e•fit•ed, ben•e•fit•ing, ben•e•fits** *or* **ben•e•fit•ted, ben•e•fit•ting, ben•e•fits.** to be useful or helpful. *Wearing glasses would benefit my ability to see.*

ben•e•fit³ /bĕn' ə fĭt/ *v.* **ben•e•fit•ed, ben•e•fit•ing, ben•e•fits** *or* **ben•e•fit•ted, ben•e•fit•ting, ben•e•fits.** to receive help. *Our dog will benefit from an obedience class.*

bib•li•og•ra•phy /bĭb' lē ŏg' rə fē/ *n., pl.* **bib•li•og•ra•phies.** a list of works on a topic. *I included a bibliography with my report on whales.* —**bib•li•o•graph•ic** *adj.* —**bib•li•o•graph•i•cal** *adj.* —**bib•li•o•graph•i•cal•ly** *adv.*

bi•og•ra•phy /bī ŏg' rə fē/ *n., pl.* **bi•og•ra•phies.** the story of a person's life written by someone else. *I read a biography of Abraham Lincoln.* —**bi•o•graph•ic** *adj.* —**bi•o•graph•i•cal** *adj.* —**bi•o•graph•i•cal•ly** *adv.*

bo•na fide /bō' nə fīd' *or* bŏn' ə fīd'/ *adj.* genuine; authentic. *The museum has a bona fide painting by Vincent van Gogh.*

bo•nan•za /bə năn' zə/ *n.* a source of great riches or profit. *The discovery of gold was a bonanza for miners.*

bo•nus /bō' nəs/ *n., pl.* **bo•nus•es.** something given in addition to what is usual or expected. *Students who read extra books were given a bonus.*

boun•te•ous /boun' tē əs/ *adj.* giving or inclined to give generously. *The corn crop was bounteous this year.*

boun•ty¹ /boun' tē/ *n., pl.* **boun•ties.** generosity in giving. *The victims of the storm depended on the bounty of the volunteers.*

boun•ty² /boun' tē/ *n., pl.* **boun•ties.** an abundant supply. *The charity received a bounty of food.*

PRONUNCIATION KEY	
/ă/	pat
/ā/	pay
/â/	care
/ä/	father
/är/	far
/ĕ/	pet
/ē/	be
/ĭ/	pit
/ī/	pie
/îr/	pier
/ŏ/	mop
/ō/	toe
/ô/	paw, for
/oi/	noise
/ou/	out
/o͝o/	look
/o͞o/	boot
/ŭ/	cut
/ûr/	urge
/th/	thin
/th/	this
/hw/	what
/zh/	vision
/ə/	about
	item
	pencil
	gallop
	circus
/ər/	butter

bril•liant¹ /brĭl′ yənt/ *adj.* shiny and bright. *I shaded my eyes from the brilliant light.* —**bril•liant•ly** *adv.* —**bril•liant•ness** *n.*

bril•liant² /brĭl′ yənt/ *adj.* very clever or intelligent. *My math professor is brilliant.* —**bril•liant•ly** *adv.* —**bril•liant•ness** *n.*

bru•tal¹ /brōōt′ l/ *adj.* cruel; showing no pity. *The brutal treatment of prisoners is wrong.* —**bru•tal•ly** *adv.*

bru•tal² /brōōt′ l/ *adj.* relentless. *The brutal cold forced us to stay inside.* —**bru•tal•ly** *adv.*

bru•tal•i•ty /brōō tăl′ ĭ tē/ *n.* the state or quality of being ruthless, cruel, or harsh. *The bully was punished for his brutality.*

cal•cu•late¹ /kăl′ kyə lāt′/ *v.* **cal•cu•lat•ed, cal•cu•lat•ing, cal•cu•lates.** to find out by using numbers. *Please calculate how much money you spend on lunch each week.*

cal•cu•late² /kăl′ kyə lāt′/ *v.* **cal•cu•lat•ed, cal•cu•lat•ing, cal•cu•lates.** to figure out; to estimate. *We calculated that it would take three hours to drive to my aunt's house.*

cal•cu•la•tion /kăl′ kyə lā′ shən/ *n.* the act, process, or result of calculating. *Our calculation for the cost of groceries was correct.*

cal•lig•ra•phy /kə lĭg′ rə fē/ *n.* fine, beautiful handwriting. *The calligraphy on the invitations was impressive.* —**cal•lig•ra•pher** *n.*

cam•paign¹ /kăm pān′/ *n.* a series of related activities organized to attain a certain goal. *The campaign for student council will begin in September.* —**cam•paign•er** *n.*

cam•paign² /kăm pān′/ *v.* **cam•paigned, cam•paign•ing, cam•paigns.** to carry on a campaign. *We campaigned for a neighborhood community center.* —**cam•paign•er** *n.*

ca•reer /kə r̂ir′/ *n.* one's chosen lifetime work or occupation; a profession. *I want to choose a career in health care.*

car•ni•vore /kär′ nə vôr′/ *n.* an animal that eats mostly meat. *At the zoo we learned that some birds, such as vultures, are carnivores.*

cha•os /kā′ ŏs′/ *n.* a state of complete disorder or great confusion. *After the earthquake, the city was in chaos.* —**cha•ot•ic** *adj.* —**cha•ot•i•cal•ly** *adv.*

chef /shĕf/ *n.* the head cook in a place that serves food. *The happy diners complimented the chef on their fine meals.*

claim¹ /klām/ *v.* **claimed, claim•ing, claims.** to ask for or demand as one's own. *The girl claimed her purse at the lost-and-found desk.*

claim² /klām/ *v.* **claimed, claim•ing, claims.** to say strongly as a fact; to declare to be true. *My friend claims she saw a two-headed snake.*

claim³ /klām/ *n.* a demand for something as one's due or right. *The man placed a claim with his insurance company for the hail damage to his car.*

cod•i•fy /kŏd′ ĭ fī′ or kō′ də fī′/ *v.* **cod•i•fied, cod•i•fy•ing, cod•i•fies.** to arrange into an organized system. *My friends and I want to codify the rules for the game we made up.* —**cod•i•fi•ca•tion** *n.* —**cod•i•fi•er** *n.*

col•lapse /kə lăps′/ *v.* **col•lapsed, col•laps•ing, col•laps•es.** to fall down suddenly. *The runner collapsed from exhaustion.* —**col•laps•i•ble** or **col•laps•a•ble** *adj.* —**col•laps•i•bil•i•ty** *n.*

com•i•cal /kŏm′ ĭ kəl/ *adj.* funny. *We couldn't stop laughing at the comical clown.* —**com•i•cal•ly** *adv.*

com•par•i•son¹ /kəm păr′ ĭ sən/ *n.* the act of examining how things are alike. *He made a comparison of this year's and last year's temperatures.*

com•par•i•son² /kəm păr′ ĭ sən/ *n.* a likeness. *There is no comparison between the baseball team's record and the football team's record.*

com•pet•i•tive /kəm pĕt′ ĭ tĭv/ *adj.* involving a competition or contest. *Tennis is a competitive sport.* —**com•pet•i•tive•ly** *adv.* —**com•pet•i•tive•ness** *n.*

com•pute /kəm pyōōt′/ *v.* **com•put•ed, com•put•ing, com•putes.** to find or work out an answer using mathematics. *I will compute the cost of a bicycle and helmet.*

con•cen•trate /kŏn′ sən trāt′/ *v.*
con•cen•trat•ed, con•cen•trat•ing,
con•cen•trates. to pay close attention or
focus one's thoughts. *It was hard to
concentrate in the noisy classroom.*

con•cept /kŏn′ sĕpt′/ *n.* a general idea, understanding, or thought based on facts or
experience. *The class learned the concept
of main ideas in paragraphs.*

con•cep•tu•al /kən sĕp′ chōō əl/ *adj.* of concepts or conception. *We learned of the
conceptual plans from the sketches.*
—**con•cep•tu•al•ly** *adv.*

con•clude¹ /kən klōōd′/ *v.* **con•clud•ed,**
con•clud•ing, con•cludes. to form an
opinion; to decide. *After hearing the facts, I
concluded that my friend did the right thing.*

con•clude² /kən klōōd′/ *v.* **con•clud•ed,**
con•clud•ing, con•cludes. to bring to an
end. *Let's conclude the concert with a
popular song.*

con•coc•tion /kən kŏk′ shən/ *n.* something
that is blended together by mixing or
combining ingredients. *Nobody would eat
our strange concoction.*

con•fec•tion /kən fĕk′ shən/ *n.* a sweet food
or mixture, such as candy. *The candy store
is famous for its wonderful confections.*

Con•gress /kŏng′ grĭs/ *n.* the lawmaking body
of the United States made up of the Senate
and the House of Representatives. *The
President and Congress worked together to
improve education.*

con•science /kŏn′ shəns/ *n.* the sense of right
and wrong that guides a person. *My
conscience won't let me cheat on a test.*

con•scious /kŏn′ shəs/ *adj.* aware of one's
own thoughts and feelings. *I was conscious
of feeling tired.* —**con•scious•ly** *adv.*

con•tain /kən tān′/ *v.* **con•tained,**
con•tain•ing, con•tains. to have in; to
hold. *Our school library contains many
interesting books.* —**con•tain•a•ble** *adj.*
—**con•tain•ment** *n.*

con•tam•i•nate /kən tăm′ ə nāt′/ *v.*
con•tam•i•nated, con•tam•i•nat•ing,
con•tam•i•nates. to pollute or make dirty
or impure. *The city checks that nothing
contaminates the drinking water.*
—**con•tam•i•na•tor** *n.*

con•tam•i•na•tion /kən tăm′ ə nā′ shən/ *n.* the
act or process of polluting or making dirty
or impure. *The dirty pond was closed due
to contamination.*

con•tract¹ /kən trăkt′ or kŏn′ trăkt/ *v.*
con•tract•ed, con•tract•ing, con•tracts.
to draw together and become smaller.
*The small rubber band contracts when I
take it off my wrist.* —**con•tract•a•ble** *adj.*
—**con•trac•tion** *n.*

con•tract² /kŏn′ trăkt/ *n.* an agreement,
that usually can be enforced by law,
between people to do or not do something.
*My parents signed a contract to buy a
new house.*

con•ven•ient¹ /kən vēn′ yənt/ *adj.* suited to
one's comfort or needs. *It is convenient
to practice the piano right after school.*
—**con•ven•ient•ly** *adv.*

con•ven•ient² /kən vēn′ yənt/ *adj.* easy to use
or reach. *We found a convenient parking
space near the restaurant.*
—**con•ven•ient•ly** *adv.*

con•ver•sa•tion•al /kŏn′ vər sā′ shə nəl/ *adj.*
like natural-sounding talk or informal
conversation. *We enjoyed the
conversational tone of the speaker.*
—**con•ver•sa•tion•al•ly** *adv.*
—**con•ver•sa•tion** *n.*

con•verse /kən vûrs′/ *v.* **con•versed,**
con•vers•ing, con•vers•es. to talk with
another person or persons. *The neighbors
often converse with one another.*

coun•ter•feit /koun′ tər fĭt′/ *adj.* not genuine.
Counterfeit money may be difficult to spot.

cri•sis /krī′ sĭs/ *n., pl.* **cri•ses** /krī′ sēz/. a time
of danger or an important decision; a
turning point. *It is difficult for most people
to be calm in a crisis.*

PRONUNCIATION KEY

/ă/	pat
/ā/	pay
/â/	care
/ä/	father
/är/	far
/ĕ/	pet
/ē/	be
/ĭ/	pit
/ī/	pie
/îr/	pier
/ŏ/	mop
/ō/	toe
/ô/	paw, for
/oi/	noise
/ou/	out
/ōō/	look
/ōō/	boot
/ŭ/	cut
/ûr/	urge
/th/	thin
/th/	this
/hw/	what
/zh/	vision
/ə/	about
	item
	pencil
	gallop
	circus
/ər/	butter

de•ceive /dĭ sēv′/ *v.* **de•ceived, de•ceiv•ing, de•ceives.** to make someone believe something that is not true; to mislead or trick. *We deceived our friend because the party was a surprise.* —**de•ceiv•a•ble** *adj.* —**de•ceiv•ing•ly** *adv.* —**de•ceiv•er** *n.*

de•clare¹ /dĭ klâr′/ *v.* **de•clared, de•clar•ing, de•clares.** to announce formally. *Our city council declared that all city parks would close at sunset.*

de•clare² /dĭ klâr′/ *v.* **de•clared, de•clar•ing, de•clares.** to state strongly. *Our teacher declared that the homework was due on Monday.*

del•e•gate /dĕl′ ĭ gāt′ or dĕl′ ĭ gĭt/ *n.* a person chosen to speak or act for others; a representative. *My teammates chose me to be their delegate at the meeting.*

del•i•ca•cy¹ /dĕl′ ĭ kə sē/ *n., pl.* **del•i•ca•cies.** a food that is considered rare or expensive. *Several delicacies were served at the wedding reception.*

del•i•ca•cy² /dĕl′ ĭ kə sē/ *n., pl.* **del•i•ca•cies.** something that is of fine quality or construction. *My grandmother is famous for the delicacy of her handmade lace.*

del•i•ca•cy³ /dĕl′ ĭ kə sē/ *n., pl.* **del•i•ca•cies.** weakness or frailty. *The doctor noticed the delicacy of the old woman's hands.*

de•moc•ra•cy /dĭ mŏk′ rə sē/ *n., pl.* **de•moc•ra•cies.** a government that is run by the people. *People have many rights in a democracy.*

de•pict /dĭ pĭkt′/ *v.* **de•pict•ed, de•pict•ing, de•picts.** to describe or show. *The stepsisters in the play were depicted as being mean.*

de•pic•tion /dĭ pĭk′ shən/ *n.* the act of describing in words. *I pictured the character based on the storyteller's depiction of her.*

de•tain /dĭ tān′/ *v.* **de•tained, de•tain•ing, de•tains.** to keep from going ahead; to delay. *I missed my bus when I was detained after school.* —**de•tain•ment** *n.*

de•trac•tor /dĭ trăkt′ ər/ *n.* a person who speaks ill of or belittles someone else. *Before the election, a detractor said bad things about the candidate.*

de•vice /dĭ vīs′/ *n.* a machine that does a particular job. *A screwdriver is a helpful device.*

de•vour¹ /dĭ vour′/ *v.* **de•voured, de•vour•ing, de•vours.** to eat greedily. *The hungry students devoured their lunches in only a few minutes.*

de•vour² /dĭ vour′/ *v.* **de•voured, de•vour•ing, de•vours.** to destroy. *The terrible fire devoured the entire forest.*

de•vour³ /dĭ vour′/ *v.* **de•voured, de•vour•ing, de•vours.** to take in greedily through the mind. *Everyone who reads the exciting book devours it.*

di•a•logue¹ /dī′ ə lôg′ or dī′ ə lŏg′/ *n.* a conversation between two or more people. *The friends had a dialogue about the game.*

di•a•logue² /dī′ ə lôg′ or dī′ ə lŏg′/ *n.* the words spoken by the actors or characters in a play or story. *The actors rehearsed their dialogue.*

dig•ni•ty¹ /dĭg′ nĭ tē/ *n., pl.* **dig•ni•ties.** the quality of being respected. *True dignity comes from who you are inside.*

dig•ni•ty² /dĭg′ nĭ tē/ *n., pl.* **dig•ni•ties.** poise and self-respect. *The senator accepted the honor with dignity.*

dis•claim /dĭs klām′/ *v.* **dis•claimed, dis•claim•ing, dis•claims.** to give up a right to, connection with, or responsibility for; to disown. *The boy disclaimed any knowledge of the broken window.*

dis•gust•ing /dĭs gus′ tĭng/ *adj.* causing feelings of strong dislike or sickening distaste. *You must clean a rabbit cage often, or it will become disgusting.* —**dis•gust•ing•ly** *adv.*

dis•mount /dĭs mount′/ *v.* **dis•mount•ed, dis•mount•ing, dis•mounts.** to get off or down. *After the parade the circus performers dismounted from the elephants.*

dis•taste•ful /dĭs tāst′ fəl/ *adj.* unpleasant; disagreeable. *I think that pulling weeds on a hot, humid day is distasteful.* —**dis•taste•ful•ly** *adv.* —**dis•taste•ful•ness** *n.*

PRONUNCIATION KEY

/ă/	pat
/ā/	pay
/â/	care
/ä/	father
/är/	far
/ĕ/	pet
/ē/	be
/ĭ/	pit
/ī/	pie
/îr/	pier
/ŏ/	mop
/ō/	toe
/ô/	paw, for
/oi/	noise
/ou/	out
/ŏŏ/	look
/ōō/	boot
/ŭ/	cut
/ûr/	urge
/th/	thin
/th/	this
/hw/	what
/zh/	vision
/ə/	about
	item
	pencil
	gallop
	circus
/ər/	butter

dis•trac•tion /dĭ străk′ shən/ *n.* something that draws attention away from something. *Loud noise in the hall was a distraction for the students in the classroom.*

doc•u•ment /dŏk′ yə mənt/ *n.* a written or printed paper that gives information, especially official or legal information. *My parents keep important documents in a safe place.*

doc•u•men•ta•ry /dŏk′ yə mĕn′ tə rē/ *n. pl.* **doc•u•men•ta•ries.** a work, such as a film, presenting its subject matter factually. *I watched the documentary for my research paper.*

drawl[1] /drôl/ *v.* **drawled, drawl•ing, drawls.** to draw out vowel sounds, slowing one's speech. *The man wearing boots and a cowboy hat drawled, "Hello, y'all."*

drawl[2] /drôl/ *n.* the manner of speech of one who drawls. *It was easy to understand the speaker's drawl.*

ef•fi•cient /ĭ fĭsh′ ənt/ *adj.* producing effectively with little effort or waste. *My brother and I are efficient when we wash the car.* —**ef•fi•cient•ly** *adv.*

e•lab•o•rate[1] /ĭ lăb′ ər ĭt/ *adj.* planned and done with great detail. *My family has elaborate vacation plans.* —**e•lab•o•rate•ly** *adv.* —**e•lab•o•rate•ness** *n.*

e•lab•o•rate[2] /ĭ lăb′ ə rāt′/ *v.* **e•lab•o•rat•ed, e•lab•o•rat•ing, e•lab•o•rates.** to provide additional information or more detail; to develop thoroughly. *The teacher asked me to elaborate on my reasons for liking the book.* —**e•lab•o•rate•ly** *adv.* —**e•lab•o•ra•tion** *n.*

em•bark /ĕm bärk′/ *v.* **em•barked, em•bark•ing, em•barks.** to begin a journey, adventure, or action. *Lewis and Clark embarked on their journey from St. Louis in 1804.* —**em•bar•ka•tion** *n.*

en•dur•ance /ĕn dŏŏr′ əns *or* ĕn dyŏŏr′ əns/ *n.* the ability to keep going in spite of harsh conditions or strain. *The endurance of the bicycle racer amazed everyone.*

en•ter•prise /ĕn′ tər prīz′/ *n.* a project, task, or undertaking, especially one that is important or difficult. *Building the first successful spacecraft was quite an enterprise.*

en•trée /ŏn′ trā *or* ŏn trā′/ *n.* the main course of a meal. *I ordered spaghetti for my entrée at the restaurant.*

e•nu•mer•ate /ĭ nŏŏ′ mə rāt′ *or* ĭ nyŏŏ′ mə rāt′/ *v.* **e•nu•mer•at•ed, e•nu•mer•at•ing, e•nu•mer•ates.** to name one by one; to list. *The girl enumerated her reasons for not cleaning her room.* —**e•nu•mer•a•tive** *adj.* —**e•nu•mer•a•tion** *n.* —**e•nu•mer•a•tor** *n.*

es•teem /ĭ stēm′/ *v.* **es•teemed, es•teem•ing, es•teems.** to respect or value. *Our class esteems our teacher.*

es•teemed /ĭ stēmd′/ *adj.* highly respected. *An esteemed athlete visited the children in the hospital.*

es•ti•mate[1] /ĕs′ tə māt′/ *v.* **es•ti•mat•ed, es•ti•mat•ing, es•ti•mates.** to make a judgment of the amount. *Our class estimated how much food an elephant eats each day.* —**es•ti•ma•tor** *n.*

es•ti•mate[2] /ĕs′ tə mĭt/ *n.* a judgment or opinion. *What is your estimate of the cost of a new bicycle?* —**es•ti•ma•tive** *adj.*

es•ti•ma•tion /ĕs′ tə mā′ shən/ *n.* the act or instance of estimating. *Was the work estimation correct?*

e•ter•ni•ty /ĭ tûr′ nĭ tē/ *n., pl.* **e•ter•ni•ties.** time without end; a long period of time that seems endless. *It seemed to take an eternity to get to my grandparents' house.*

e•val•u•ate /ĭ văl′ yŏŏ āt′/ *v.* **e•val•u•at•ed, e•val•u•at•ing, e•val•u•ates.** to determine the worth or value of something. *I would like someone to evaluate the story that I wrote.* —**e•val•u•a•tion** *n.* —**e•val•u•a•tor** *n.*

ex•cerpt[1] /ĕk′ sûrpt′/ *n.* a part taken from a longer work. *We memorized an excerpt from the play.*

ex•cerpt[2] /ĭk´ sûrpt´/ *v.* **ex•cerpt•ed, ex•cerpt•ing, ex•cerpts.** to use a passage from a longer work. *Our teacher excerpted paragraphs from the story.*

ex•cess /ĭk sĕs´ *or* ĕk´ sĕs´/ *n.* the state of exceeding what is normal or sufficient. *I ate to excess at the party.*

ex•claim /ĭk sklām´/ *v.* **ex•claimed, ex•claim•ing, ex•claims.** to speak, call, or shout out suddenly or with force, often in surprise. *"Wow!" the children exclaimed when the magician pulled the rabbit out of a hat.*

ex•ert /ĭg zûrt´/ *v.* **ex•ert•ed, ex•ert•ing, ex•erts.** to put (oneself) to a great effort. *During football practice, all of the team members exert themselves.* —**ex•er•tion** *n.*

ex•pres•sion[1] /ĭk sprĕsh´ ən/ *n.* the act of communicating, as in words. *Pam's speech was an expression of her ideas.*

ex•pres•sion[2] /ĭk sprĕsh´ ən/ *n.* something that communicates. *The flowers were an expression of our sorrow.*

ex•pres•sion[3] /ĭk sprĕsh´ ən/ *n.* a look that shows feelings. *Jordan's serious expression meant things were going badly.*

ex•pres•sion[4] /ĭk sprĕsh´ ən/ *n.* a way of speaking, singing, or playing that shows a certain feeling. *Our teacher read the poem with great expression.*

ex•pres•sion[5] /ĭk sprĕsh´ ən/ *n.* a particular word or phrase. *I hear the expression "Exercise your right to vote" around election day.*

ex•tract[1] /ĭk străkt´/ *v.* **ex•tract•ed, ex•tract•ing, ex•tracts.** to pull or draw out with force or effort. *We had to extract a tiny, sharp rock from our dog's paw.* —**ex•tract•a•ble** *or* **ex•tract•i•ble** *adj.* —**ex•trac•tion** *n.*

ex•tract[2] /ĕk´ străkt´/ *n.* a portion of a book or magazine. *Our class read an extract from the book.*

ex•tract[3] /ĕk´ străkt´/ *n.* a concentrated flavoring. *I used vanilla extract in the cake.*

fa•tigue /fə tēg´/ *n.* a tired feeling; weariness as a result of effort. *The long hike caused great fatigue in all of the campers.*

fea•ture /fē´ chər/ *n.* a distinct quality or characteristic. *The lake is an outstanding feature of the landscape.*

fea•ture•less /fē´ chər lĭs/ *adj.* lacking distinct parts or qualities. *Anything more than a few feet away appeared featureless in the fog.*

fed•er•al /fĕd´ ər əl *or* fĕd´ rəl/ *adj.* of or relating to the central government of a country. *The federal government is in charge of national security.* —**fed•er•al•ly** *adv.*

fic•tion /fĭk´ shən/ *n.* something that is made up. *The events in the story were fiction.* —**fic•tion•al** *adj.* —**fic•tion•al•ly** *adv.*

fig•u•ra•tive /fĭg´ yər ə tĭv/ *adj.* using imaginative comparisons to express an idea or thought. *A poet uses figurative language to create a certain effect.* —**fig•u•ra•tive•ly** *adv.* —**fig•u•ra•tive•ness** *n.*

flail /flāl/ *v.* **flailed, flail•ing, flails.** to wave or swing with power or force. *When I was learning to ice skate, I flailed my arms to keep from losing my balance.*

fla•vor•ful /flā´ vər fəl/ *adj.* full of flavor, tasty. *All of my friends complimented the flavorful scrambled eggs.* —**fla•vor•ful•ly** *adv.*

folk•lore /fōk´ lôr´ *or* fōk´ lōr´/ *n.* the stories, songs, and practices handed down among a people. *The folklore of the Old West can be very entertaining.* —**folk•lor•ic** *adj.* —**folk•lor•ist** *n.*

for•feit /fôr´ fĭt/ *v.* **for•feit•ed, for•feit•ing, for•feits.** to lose or give up the right to something as a penalty. *The basketball team had to forfeit the game.*

for•mer•ly /fôr´ mər lē/ *adv.* at an earlier time; once. *She was formerly a teacher.*

for•mu•late /fôr´ myə lāt´/ *v.* **for•mu•lat•ed, for•mu•lat•ing, for•mu•lates.** to plan in a clear, orderly way. *Let's formulate our plans for the birthday party.* —**for•mu•la•tion** *n.*

fo•rum /fôr´ əm *or* fōr´ əm/ *n., pl.* **fo•rums.** a place to meet and discuss issues. *City council held a forum to discuss the proposal.*

fric•tion /frĭk´ shən/ *n.* the rubbing of one object or surface against another. *I created friction by rubbing the wood with sandpaper.* —**fric•tion•al** *adj.* —**fric•tion•al•ly** *adv.*

frig·id /frĭj′ ĭd/ *adj.* extremely cold. *Canadian winters are frigid.* —**frig·id·ly** *adv.* —**frig·id·ness** *n.*

gen·re /zhän′ rə/ *n.* a particular type of literature or art. *Mysteries are a popular genre in literature and film.*

graph·ic /grăf′ ĭk/ *adj.* described in clear detail. *The newspaper article gave a graphic report of the accident.* —**graph·i·cal·ly** *adv.* —**graph·ic·ness** *n.*

haz·ard·ous /hăz′ ər dəs/ *adj.* dangerous. *During the heavy snowstorm, driving was hazardous.* —**haz·ard·ous·ly** *adv.* —**haz·ard·ous·ness** *n.*

hem·i·sphere /hĕm′ ĭ sfîr′/ *n.* the northern or southern half of the earth's surface. *We studied some of the animals that live in the northern hemisphere.* —**hem·i·spher·ic** *adj.* —**hem·i·spher·i·cal** *adj.* —**hem·i·spher·i·cal·ly** *adv.*

her·bi·vore /hûr′ bə vôr′ *or* ûr′ bə vôr′/ *n.* an animal that eats mostly plants. *Many herbivores, such as cows and horses, live on farms.*

hom·o·nym /hŏm′ ə nĭm′ *or* hō′ mə nĭm′/ *n.* a word that sounds the same as another word but has a different meaning and often a different spelling. *The words* our *and* hour *are homonyms.*

hu·man·i·tar·i·an[1] /hyōō măn′ ĭ târ′ ē ən/ *n.* a person who shows concern for the well-being of people. *A humanitarian spoke to our class about ways to help other people.*

hu·man·i·tar·i·an[2] /hyōō măn′ ĭ târ′ ē ən/ *adj.* showing concern for the well-being of people. *She was honored for her humanitarian work in our community.*

hu·mil·i·ate /hyōō mĭl′ ē āt′/ *v.* **hu·mil·i·at·ed, hu·mil·i·at·ing, hu·mil·i·ates.** to lower the pride or dignity of. *I did not mean to humiliate my friend.*

hu·mil·i·a·tion /hyōō mĭl′ ē ā′ shən/ *n.* the condition of shame or disgrace. *He blushed from the humiliation.*

hu·mor·ist /hyōō′ mər ĭst/ *n.* someone who performs or writes funny material. *The humorist was the star of the show.*

hur·tle /hûr′ tl/ *v.* **hur·tled, hur·tling, hur·tles.** to move very fast, often with noise. *The horses hurtled toward us when they saw us come into the pasture.*

i·den·ti·fy /ī dĕn′ tə fī′/ *v.* **i·den·ti·fied, i·den·ti·fy·ing, i·den·ti·fies.** to recognize and name as being a particular person or thing. *We could identify our lost dog as soon as we saw her.* —**i·den·ti·fi·a·ble** *adj.*

id·i·om /ĭd′ ē əm/ *n.* an expression whose meaning cannot be understood from the usual meanings of the words in it. *"You're pulling my leg" is an idiom meaning "You're not telling me the truth."*

id·i·o·mat·ic /ĭd′ ē ə măt′ ĭk/ *adj.* peculiar to or characteristic of a given language. *Idiomatic phrases are not often found in lectures.*

il·le·gal[1] /ĭ lē′ gəl/ *adj.* not allowed by law. *It is illegal to litter along the highway.*

il·le·gal[2] /ĭ lē′ gəl/ *adj.* not allowed by the official rules, as in sports. *Our team was penalized for the illegal delay of game.*

im·per·son·ate /ĭm pûr′ sə nāt′/ *v.* **im·per·son·at·ed, im·per·son·at·ing, im·per·son·ates.** to act like or copy the appearance or speech of another person. *As a joke, the student tried to impersonate his teacher.*

im·ple·ment[1] /ĭm′ plə mĕnt′/ *v.* **im·ple·ment·ed, im·ple·ment·ing, im·ple·ments.** to put into effect; to carry out. *This year our school has implemented a new lunch schedule.* —**im·ple·men·ta·tion** *n.*

im·ple·ment[2] /ĭm′ plə mənt/ *n.* a tool used in doing a job or task. *Computer stores sell implements for cleaning keyboards.*

PRONUNCIATION KEY	
/ă/	pat
/ā/	pay
/â/	care
/ä/	father
/är/	far
/ĕ/	pet
/ē/	be
/ĭ/	pit
/ī/	pie
/îr/	pier
/ŏ/	mop
/ō/	toe
/ô/	paw, for
/oi/	noise
/ou/	out
/ŏŏ/	look
/ōō/	boot
/ŭ/	cut
/ûr/	urge
/th/	thin
/th/	this
/hw/	what
/zh/	vision
/ə/	about
	item
	pencil
	gallop
	circus
/ər/	butter

in•de•ci•sive /ĭn′ dĭ sī′ sĭv/ *adj.* not able to make up one's mind. *The driver was indecisive about which way to turn.* —**in•de•ci•sive•ly** *adv.* —**in•de•ci•sive•ness** *n.*

in•fer /ĭn fûr′/ *v.* **in•ferred, in•fer•ring, in•fers.** to conclude from thinking carefully about the evidence. *Because you are wearing a coat, I infer that it is cold outside.*

in•flate¹ /ĭn flāt′/ *v.* **in•flat•ed, in•flat•ing, in•flates.** to expand by filling with air or gas. *We will inflate balloons for the party.*

in•flate² /ĭn flāt′/ *v.* **in•flat•ed, in•flat•ing, in•flates.** to increase beyond normal levels. *Do businesses inflate prices when there is a large demand for their products?*

in•fla•tion /ĭn flā′ shən/ *n.* the act of inflating or the state of being inflated. *The inflation of the tire made riding the bike easier.*

in•gen•ious /ĭn jēn′ yəs/ *adj.* clever; imaginative. *The ingenious squirrel hid the acorn in the flowerpot.* —**in•gen•ious•ly** *adv.* —**in•gen•ious•ness** *n.*

in•sa•tia•ble /ĭn sā′ shə bəl *or* ĭn sā′ shē ə bəl/ *adj.* not able to be satisfied. *We feed our puppy often because she has an insatiable appetite.* —**in•sa•tia•bly** *adv.* —**in•sa•tia•bil•i•ty** *or* **in•sa•tia•ble•ness** *n.*

in•sight /ĭn′ sīt′/ *n.* the ability to see the true nature of something. *Mom has insight into what I mean even when I say only a few words.*

in•sight•ful /ĭn′ sīt′ fəl/ *adj.* showing or having insight; perceptive. *Her criticism of the movie was insightful.* —**in•sight•ful•ly** *adv.*

in•sip•id¹ /ĭn sĭp′ ĭd/ *adj.* without much flavor or taste. *The guests tried to eat the insipid vegetables just to be polite.* —**in•sip•id•ly** *adv.* —**in•sip•id•ness** *n.*

in•sip•id² /ĭn sĭp′ ĭd/ *adj.* not having much interest; dull. *I decided not to finish reading the insipid book.* —**in•sip•id•ly** *adv.* —**in•sip•id•ness** *n.*

in•sist /ĭn sĭst′/ *v.* **in•sist•ed, in•sist•ing, in•sists.** to take a firm stand; to demand. *My mother insisted that I go to bed early.* —**in•sis•tence** *n.*

in•stinct¹ /ĭn′ stĭngkt′/ *n.* a natural tendency to act in a certain way. *It is an instinct in many animals to run and hide from danger.*

in•stinct² /ĭn′ stĭngkt′/ *n.* an inborn ability. *My brother has an instinct for playing music.*

in•tend /ĭn tĕnd′/ *v.* **in•tend•ed, in•tend•ing, in•tends.** to have a purpose in mind; to plan. *We intend to take the bus to the game.*

in•ter•pret¹ /ĭn tûr′ prĭt/ *v.* **in•ter•pret•ed, in•ter•pret•ing, in•ter•prets.** to explain the meaning of. *It takes an expert to interpret the marks on the ancient tomb.*

in•ter•pret² /ĭn tûr′ prĭt/ *v.* **in•ter•pret•ed, in•ter•pret•ing, in•ter•prets.** to understand. *I am able to interpret sign language.*

in•ter•pre•tive /ĭn tûr′ prĭ tĭv/ *adj.* relating to or marked by interpretation; explanatory. *I practiced my interpretive dance routine.* —**in•ter•pre•tive•ly** *adv.*

in•to•na•tion /ĭn′ tə nā′ shən/ *n.* the rise and fall in pitch of the voice. *Good intonation is important in public speaking.*

in•ves•ti•gate /ĭn vĕs′ tĭ gāt′/ *v.* **in•ves•ti•gat•ed, in•ves•ti•gat•ing, in•ves•ti•gates.** to examine closely to learn the truth. *Police often investigate automobile accidents.*

judg•ment¹ /jŭj′ mənt/ *n.* an opinion or conclusion made after careful thought. *In my judgment, there should be a traffic light at that corner.*

judg•ment² /jŭj′ mənt/ *n.* a decision, order, or sentence given in a court of law. *The jury member read the judgment to the court.*

ju•di•cial /jōō dĭsh′ əl/ *adj.* of or by judges or courts of law. *The judicial decision on the law was reported in the news.* —**ju•di•cial•ly** *adv.*

jus•tice /jŭs′ tĭs/ *n.* fairness. *The judge handed down her orders with justice.*

jus•ti•fy /jŭs′ tə fī′/ *v.* **jus•ti•fied, jus•ti•fy•ing, jus•ti•fies.** to show or prove to be correct or fair. *A beautiful summer garden will justify our hard work in the spring.*

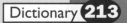

lec•ture¹ /lĕk′ chər/ *n.* a planned talk on a specific subject given to an audience. *The famous artist gave a lecture about her paintings.*

lec•ture² /lĕk′ chər/ *n.* a serious talk or scolding. *Our teacher gave us a lecture about being tardy.*

lec•ture³ /lĕk′ chər/ *v.* **lec•tured, lec•tur•ing, lec•tures.** to give a lecture. *The professor lectured on ancient Greek history.*

lec•ture⁴ /lĕk′ chər/ *v.* **lec•tured, lec•tur•ing, lec•tures.** to scold. *Parents sometimes lecture their children.*

le•gal•ize /lē′ gə līz′/ *v.* **le•gal•ized, le•gal•iz•ing, le•gal•iz•es.** to make lawful. *The government legalized the selling of medicine without a prescription.* —**le•gal•i•za•tion** *n.*

le•git•i•mate¹ /lə jĭt′ ə mĭt/ *adj.* allowed by law. *The accident victim made a legitimate claim.* —**le•git•i•mate•ly** *adv.*

le•git•i•mate² /lə jĭt′ ə mĭt/ *adj.* reasonable; valid. *The student had a legitimate reason for being tardy.* —**le•git•i•mate•ly** *adv.*

lib•er•ty /lĭb′ ər tē/ *n., pl.* **lib•er•ties.** freedom. *Citizens of the United States have the liberty to travel throughout the country.*

lit•er•al /lĭt′ ər əl/ *adj.* the exact or factual meaning of words. *Help me explain the literal meaning of that phrase.* —**lit•er•al•ly** *adv.* —**lit•er•al•ness** *n.*

lit•er•ate /lĭt′ ər ĭt/ *adj.* able to read and write. *The author who visited our class is a highly literate person.* —**lit•er•ate•ly** *adv.* —**lit•er•ate•ness** *n.*

lit•er•a•ture /lĭt′ ər ə choor′ *or* lĭt′ ər ə chər/ *n.* written works that show imagination and have lasting value. *Good children's literature is also enjoyed by adults.*

log•i•cal /lŏj′ ĭ kəl/ *adj.* based on clear thinking. *Everyone understood the logical answer to the question.* —**log•i•cal•ly** *adv.*

lon•gi•tude /lŏn′ jĭ tood′ *or* lŏn′ jĭ tyood′/ *n.* distance on the earth's surface, measured east or west from the prime meridian. *Ship captains track their longitude to keep on course.*

main•tain¹ /mān tān′/ *v.* **main•tained, main•tain•ing, main•tains.** to keep in good condition. *Because our neighbors were too busy to maintain their big house, they decided to move to a smaller one.* —**main•tain•a•ble** *adj.* —**main•tain•er** *n.*

main•tain² /mān tān′/ *v.* **main•tained, main•tain•ing, main•tains.** to continue or keep up. *Whenever they can, drivers should maintain a constant speed.* —**main•tain•a•ble** *adj.* —**main•tain•er** *n.*

mal•treat•ment /măl trēt′ mənt/ *n.* cruel or rough action; abuse. *The people were arrested for the maltreatment of their dog.*

man•age•ment /măn′ ĭj mənt/ *n.* the act or practice of directing or operating. *The management of an airport must be a difficult job.*

ma•neu•ver¹ /mə noo′ vər *or* mə nyoo′ vər/ *v.* **ma•neu•vered, ma•neu•ver•ing, ma•neu•vers.** to move with skill, ability, or cleverness. *My aunt maneuvered her car into the small parking space.*

ma•neu•ver² /mə noo′ vər *or* mə nyoo′ vər/ *n.* a skillful or well-planned move. *The quarterback's quick maneuver won his team the game.*

mar•a•thon¹ /măr′ ə thŏn′/ *n.* a footrace that covers 26 miles, 385 yards (41.3 kilometers). *The runner trained for a year to get in shape for the marathon.*

mar•a•thon² /măr′ ə thŏn′/ *n.* any race or contest that lasts a long time. *The high school had a dance marathon that lasted all night.*

mas•sive /măs′ ĭv/ *adj.* having great size and weight. *It was difficult to move the massive furniture.* —**mas•sive•ly** *adv.* —**mas•sive•ness** *n.*

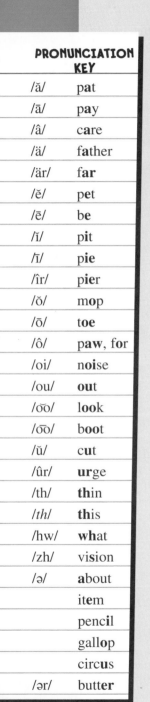

PRONUNCIATION KEY	
/ă/	pat
/ā/	pay
/â/	care
/ä/	father
/är/	far
/ĕ/	pet
/ē/	be
/ĭ/	pit
/ī/	pie
/îr/	pier
/ŏ/	mop
/ō/	toe
/ô/	paw, for
/oi/	noise
/ou/	out
/oo/	look
/oo/	boot
/ŭ/	cut
/ûr/	urge
/th/	thin
/th/	this
/hw/	what
/zh/	vision
/ə/	about
	item
	pencil
	gallop
	circus
/ər/	butter

merg•er /mûr′ jər/ *n.* the bringing together to become one, especially of two or more businesses. *The merger of the two small neighborhood markets resulted in one large grocery store.*

me•thod•i•cal /mə thŏd′ ĭ kəl/ *adj.* in a set order; according to plan. *My family cleans the house in a methodical manner.* —**me•thod•i•cal•ly** *adv.*

mi•cro•scop•ic /mī′ krə **skŏp**′ ĭk/ *adj.* tiny but able to be seen through a microscope. *Microscopic bits of dust float in the air.* —**mi•cro•scop•i•cal•ly** *adv.*

mon•o•logue¹ /mŏn′ ə lôg′ *or* mŏn′ ə lŏg′/ *n.* the series of stories and jokes told by a comedian. *The audience laughed at the funny monologue.*

mon•o•logue² /mŏn′ ə lôg′ *or* mŏn′ ə lŏg′/ *n.* a long speech by a performer. *My part in the play was to recite a monologue.*

mon•o•tone /mŏn′ ə tōn′/ *n.* a series of words or sounds uttered in one tone of voice. *We got sleepy listening to the speaker's monotone.*

muse /myōōz/ *v.* **mused, mus•ing, mus•es.** to think or consider deeply, especially in a dreamy way. *Many young people muse about what they will do when they grow up.*

nav•i•gate /năv′ ĭ gāt′/ *v.* **nav•i•gat•ed, nav•i•gat•ing, nav•i•gates.** to plan the path of and guide a boat or an airplane. *Columbus navigated the unknown waters of the Atlantic Ocean.* —**nav•i•ga•tion** *n.*

ne•go•ti•a•tion /nĭ gō′ shē ā′ shən/ *n.* the process of reaching agreement through discussion and debate. *Our negotiations for a lower price on a new car were successful.* —**ne•go•ti•a•tor** *n.*

no•tion /nō′ shən/ *n.* an idea; a belief or opinion. *Everyone listened quietly to the man's notion about why cats are good pets.*

nour•ish¹ /nûr′ ĭsh *or* nŭr′ ĭsh/ *v.* **nour•ished, nour•ish•ing, nou•rish•es.** to give food or other things that are needed for life. *We nourish our cat with food that the veterinarian said to use.* —**nou•rish•er** *n.*

nour•ish² /nûr′ ĭsh *or* nŭr′ ĭsh/ *v.* **nour•ished, nour•ish•ing, nour•ish•es.** to support and help the growth or development of. *My friends and I nourish our friendship by listening to each other.* —**nou•rish•er** *n.*

nour•ish•ment /nûr′ ĭsh mənt/ *n.* the act of supporting and helping the growth or development of. *I added plant food to my flower for nourishment.*

nu•tri•ent /nōō′ trē ənt *or* nyōō′ trē ənt/ *n.* something that supports and helps growth or development, especially an ingredient in food. *My parents read food labels to find foods rich in nutrients.*

nu•tri•tious /nōō trĭsh′ əs *or* nyōō trĭsh′ əs/ *adj.* nourishing. *It is important to begin the day with a nutritious breakfast.* —**nu•tri•tious•ly** *adv.* —**nu•tri•tious•ness** *n.*

op•por•tu•ni•ty /ŏp′ ər tōō′ nĭ tē *or* ŏp′ ər tyōō′ nĭ tē/ *n., pl.* **op•por•tu•ni•ties.** a time or circumstance suitable for a particular purpose; a chance. *I had the opportunity to get an autograph from my favorite baseball player.*

or•deal /ôr dēl′/ *n.* a difficult or painful experience. *Reporters asked the survivors of the tornado to tell about their ordeal.*

out•come /out′ kŭm′/ *n.* the final result. *The outcome of the student council election will be announced tomorrow.*

pal•at•a•ble¹ /păl′ ə tə bəl/ *adj.* agreeable enough to the taste to be eaten. *Usually my sister's cooking is palatable, so I do not complain when she cooks dinner.* —**pal•at•a•bly** *adv.* —**pal•at•a•bil•i•ty** *n.* —**pal•at•a•ble•ness** *n.*

pal•at•a•ble² /păl′ ə tə bəl/ *adj.* agreeable to the mind. *His suggestion for the game was palatable to everyone.* —**pal•at•a•bly** *adv.* —**pal•at•a•bil•i•ty** *n.* —**pal•at•a•ble•ness** *n.*

pa•tri•ot•ic /pā′ trē ŏt′ ĭk/ *adj.* feeling or showing love for one's country. *Many patriotic people fly flags on the Fourth of July.* —**pa•tri•ot•i•cal•ly** *adv.*

per•cep•tion /pər sĕp′ shən/ *n.* the power or act of becoming aware by using the senses; awareness. *Without my glasses, my perception of details is a little off.*

per•son•nel /pûr′ sə nĕl′/ *n.* the people working for a business or other organization. *The bank's personnel meet once a month.*

pe•ti•tion¹ /pə tĭsh′ ən/ *n.* a formal written request to someone in authority. *Everyone signed a petition calling for new textbooks.*

pe•ti•tion² /pə tĭsh′ ən/ *v.* **pe•ti•tioned, pe•ti•tion•ing, pe•ti•tions.** to make a formal request to someone in authority. *Voters petitioned their state representatives to lower taxes.*

plen•ti•ful /plĕn′ tĭ fəl/ *adj.* more than enough; abundant. *At the beginning of the school year, we had a plentiful supply of chalk.* —**plen•ti•ful•ly** *adv.* —**plen•ti•ful•ness** *n.*

plod¹ /plŏd/ *v.* **plod•ded, plod•ding, plods.** to work or act slowly or wearily, but steadily. *I plodded through the hard problems.* —**plod•ding•ly** *adv.* —**plod•der** *n.*

plod² /plŏd/ *v.* **plod•ded, plod•ding, plods.** to walk with great effort. *The men had to plod through the mud to rescue the dog.* —**plod•ding•ly** *adv.* —**plod•der** *n.*

pos•i•tive¹ /pŏz′ ĭ tĭv/ *adj.* focusing on favorable things. *The teacher's positive comments made the class happy.* —**pos•i•tive•ly** *adv.* —**pos•i•tive•ness** *n.*

pos•i•tive² /pŏz′ ĭ tĭv/ *adj.* certain; sure. *I am positive that my friend lives next to the park.* —**pos•i•tive•ly** *adv.* —**pos•i•tive•ness** *n.*

pre•con•ceive /prē′ kən sēv′/ *v.* **pre•con•ceived, pre•con•ceiv•ing, pre•con•ceives.** to form an opinion or idea of beforehand. *I'll preconceive the speech before I write it.* —**pre•con•ceived** *adj.*

prej•u•dice¹ /prĕj′ ə dĭs/ *n.* an unfair opinion that is made before one knows the facts. *My sister is a dog lover, but she shows no prejudice against cats.*

prej•u•dice² /prĕj′ ə dĭs/ *v.* **prej•u•diced, prej•u•dic•ing, prej•u•dic•es.** to cause to form an unfavorable decision before having all the facts. *My friend's opinion of the new restaurant prejudiced me against it.*

prep•a•ra•tion /prĕp′ ə rā′ shən/ *n.* the act of getting ready. *The preparation of a holiday meal may take a great deal of time.*

prin•ci•ple /prĭn′ sə pəl/ *n.* a basic truth; a rule. *A principle of good manners is to be thoughtful of other people.*

prob•a•ble /prŏb′ ə bəl/ *adj.* likely to be true or to happen. *It is probable that it will rain tomorrow.* —**prob•a•bly** *adv.*

probe¹ /prōb/ *v.* **probed, prob•ing, probes.** to investigate, examine, or explore. *Geologists probed the mineral makeup of the rock.*

probe² /prōb/ *n.* an investigation or exploration. *The reporter's in-depth probe led to new school reforms.*

pro•claim /prə klām′ *or* prō klām′/ *v.* **pro•claimed, pro•claim•ing, pro•claims.** to declare, make known, or announce officially. *The principal proclaimed the first Monday of each month as Reading for Fun Day.*

pro•fes•sion•al¹ /prə fĕsh′ ə nəl/ *adj.* doing specific work for pay or as a career. *The professional singer just recorded a new song.* —**pro•fes•sion•al•ly** *adv.*

pro•fes•sion•al² /prə fĕsh′ ə nəl/ *adj.* having or doing specific work with great skill. *The students in the school play gave a professional performance.* —**pro•fes•sion•al•ly** *adv.*

pro•fes•sion•al³ /prə fĕsh′ ə nəl/ *n.* a person who is skilled or expert in specific work. *My aunt sews clothes like a professional.* —**pro•fes•sion•al•ly** *adv.*

prof•it¹ /prŏf′ ĭt/ *n.* the money made in a business after the costs and expenses have been paid. *I made a profit cutting grass last summer.* —**prof•it•a•ble** *adj.* —**prof•it•a•bly** *adv.* —**prof•it•a•bil•i•ty** *n.*

prof•it² /prŏf′ ĭt/ *v.* **prof•it•ed, prof•it•ing, prof•its.** to get something helpful; to gain. *We profited from the guest speaker's advice.* —**prof•it•a•ble** *adj.* —**prof•it•a•bly** *adv.* —**prof•it•a•bil•i•ty** *n.*

PRONUNCIATION KEY	
/ă/	pat
/ā/	pay
/â/	care
/ä/	father
/är/	far
/ĕ/	pet
/ē/	be
/ĭ/	pit
/ī/	pie
/îr/	pier
/ŏ/	mop
/ō/	toe
/ô/	paw, for
/oi/	noise
/ou/	out
/ŏŏ/	look
/ōō/	boot
/ŭ/	cut
/ûr/	urge
/th/	thin
/th/	this
/hw/	what
/zh/	vision
/ə/	about
	item
	pencil
	gallop
	circus
/ər/	butter

pro•logue /prō′ lôg′ *or* prō′ lŏg′/ *n.* an introduction to a book, a play, a poem, or an opera. *Our teacher read the prologue of the play.*

pro•nounce•ment /prə nouns′ mənt/ *n.* a formal opinion or decision. *Do you agree with the judge's pronouncement?*

pro•pose /prə pōz′/ *v.* **pro•posed, pro•pos•ing, pro•pos•es.** to put forward for discussion; to suggest. *Everyone in the class had to propose an idea for a field trip.*

pros•per /prŏs′ pər/ *v.* **pros•pered, pros•per•ing, pros•pers.** to be successful; to thrive. *Good growing conditions help farmers prosper.*

pro•tag•o•nist /prō tăg′ ə nĭst/ *n.* the main character in a story, book, or play. *The protagonist of the story was a young boy.*

pro•test¹ /prō′ tĕst′/ *n.* disapproval; objection. *The governor heard the protests about the bill and decided not to sign it.*

pro•test² /prə tĕst′ *or* prō′ tĕst′/ *v.* **pro•test•ed, pro•test•ing, pro•tests.** to express strong disapproval or objection to something. *The workers protested their low wages.* —**pro•test•ing•ly** *adv.* —**pro•test•er** *n.*

pro•tract /prō trăkt′ *or* prə trăkt′/ *v.* **pro•tract•ed, pro•tract•ing, pro•tracts.** to lengthen in time; to draw out. *I would like to protract summer vacation.* —**pro•trac•tion** *n.*

pro•trac•tor /prō trăk′ tər/ *n.* a semicircular instrument for measuring and constructing angles. *I need to bring my protractor to math class.*

pseu•do•nym /sōōd′ n ĭm′/ *n.* a made-up name used by an author. *Dr. Seuss is the pseudonym of Theodor Geisel.*

pub•lish /pŭb′ lĭsh/ *v.* **pub•lished, pub•lish•ing, pub•lish•es.** to produce or print for sale or to give away. *Our school's parent organization plans to publish a cookbook.* —**pub•lish•a•ble** *adj.*

pur•pose /pûr′ pəs/ *n.* the planned or desired result; goal. *The purpose of batting practice is to improve the team's hitting.* —**pur•pose•ly** *adv.*

pur•pose•ful /pûr′ pəs fəl/ *adj.* having a purpose; determined. *My goal is to live a purposeful life.* —**pur•pose•ful•ly** *adv.*

pu•trid¹ /pyōō′ trĭd/ *adj.* decayed and having an unpleasant smell. *I immediately placed the putrid fish into the garbage.* —**pu•trid•ly** *adv.* —**pu•trid•ness** *n.*

pu•trid² /pyōō′ trĭd/ *adj.* caused by something being decayed or rotten. *The putrid smell of the dead animal filled the campsite.* —**pu•trid•ly** *adv.* —**pu•trid•ness** *n.*

quip /kwĭp/ *n.* a clever, witty remark. *My friend's quip made everyone laugh.*

ran•cid /răn′ sĭd/ *adj.* having the unpleasant smell or taste of something spoiled. *Food left out of the refrigerator becomes rancid in a short time.* —**ran•cid•ly** *adv.* —**ran•cid•ness** *n.*

re•act /rē ăkt′/ *v.* **re•act•ed, re•act•ing, re•acts.** to act back or respond to something. *When the telephone rings, people react by answering it.*

re•cline /rĭ klīn′/ *v.* **re•clined, re•clin•ing, re•clines.** to lie back or down. *I reclined on the sofa to watch the movie.*

re•duce /rĭ dōōs′ *or* rĭ dyōōs′/ *v.* **re•duced, re•duc•ing, re•duc•es.** to make less or smaller; to decrease. *The salesperson reduced the price of the car.*

re•pair /rĭ pâr′/ *v.* **re•paired, re•pair•ing, re•pairs.** to fix or mend. *The bicycle shop will repair any kind of bicycle.*

rep•a•ra•ble /rĕp′ ər ə bəl/ *adj.* able to be fixed or mended. *The torn baseball glove is reparable.* —**rep•a•ra•bly** *adv.* —**rep•a•ra•bil•i•ty** *n.*

rep•re•sen•ta•tive /rĕp′ rĭ zĕn′ tə tĭv/ *n.* a person who is appointed, elected, or chosen to act for others. *Each class elects one representative to meet with the principal once a month.*

re•solve¹ /rĭ zŏlv′/ *v.* **re•solved, re•solv•ing, re•solves.** to find a solution to. *We were able to resolve our argument.*

re•solve² /rĭ zŏlv′/ *n.* firmness of purpose; resolution. *I am following my resolve to exercise more.*

re•tain /rĭ tān′/ *v.* **re•tained, re•tain•ing, re•tains.** to keep; to hold onto. *A good teacher retains the ability to talk with students.* —**re•tain•a•ble** *adj.* —**re•tain•ment** *n.*

rid•i•cule¹ /rĭd′ ĭ kyool′/ *v.* **rid•i•culed, rid•i•cul•ing, rid•i•cules.** to make fun of. *Do not ridicule people when they make mistakes.*

rid•i•cule² /rĭd′ ĭ kyool′/ *n.* words or actions intended to make fun of a person or thing. *The girl's feelings were hurt by her friend's ridicule.*

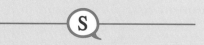

sal•a•ry /săl′ ə rē *or* săl′ rē/ *n., pl.* **sal•a•ries.** regular payment for a job. *My mother earns a good salary from her job.*

sa•ti•ate /sā′ shē āt′/ *v.* **sa•ti•at•ed, sa•ti•at•ing, sa•ti•ates.** to satisfy a hunger or desire completely. *The glass of lemonade helps satiate my thirst.* —**sa•ti•a•tion** *n.*

sa•ti•a•tion /sā′ shē ā′ shən/ *n.* the state of being completely satisfied. *The movie's happy ending left me in a state of satiation.*

sat•u•rate¹ /săch′ ə rāt′/ *v.* **sat•u•rat•ed, sat•u•rat•ing, sat•u•rates.** to completely soak. *The water from the hurricane saturated the coastline.* —**sat•u•ra•ble** *adj.* —**sat•u•ra•tor** *n.*

sat•u•rate² /săch′ ə rāt′/ *v.* **sat•u•rat•ed, sat•u•rat•ing, sat•u•rates.** to fill totally. *The firefighters began to cough as smoke saturated their lungs.* —**sat•u•ra•ble** *adj.* —**sat•u•ra•tor** *n.*

sat•u•ra•tion /săch′ ə rā′ shən/ *n.* the act or process of being filled totally. *The sponge was heavy with saturation.*

sa•vor /sā′ vər/ *v.* **sa•vored, sa•vor•ing, sa•vors.** to taste with enjoyment. *We savored the first homegrown tomatoes of the summer.* —**sa•vor•ous** *adj.* —**sa•vor•er** *n.*

sa•vor•y /sā′ və rē/ *adj.* agreeable in taste or smell; appetizing. *When we smelled the savory bread, we knew that dinner would be good.*

sci•en•tif•ic /sī′ ən tĭf′ ĭk/ *adj.* based on careful, systematic study. *Doctors know about the human body because of scientific research.* —**sci•en•tif•i•cal•ly** *adv.*

sim•i•le /sĭm′ ə lē/ *n.* a comparison of two different things, usually with *like* or *as.* "*The fog is like a blanket over the road*" *is a simile.*

site /sīt/ *n.* a place where something is or happens; a setting. *The school carnival is held at the same site every year.*

sole /sōl/ *adj.* only one; single. *The boy's sole reason for going to the game was to see his friends.*

sol•i•tar•y /sŏl′ ĭ tĕr′ ē/ *adj.* alone. *Reading is a solitary but enjoyable pastime.* —**sol•i•tar•i•ly** *adv.* —**sol•i•tar•i•ness** *n.*

sol•i•tude /sŏl′ ĭ tood′ *or* sŏl′ ĭ tyood′/ *n.* the state of being alone. *Solitude allows me to think about many things.*

so•lo•ist /sō′ lō ĭst/ *n.* a person who acts or performs alone. *The piano soloist played music written by Mozart.*

so•phis•ti•cat•ed¹ /sə fĭs′ tĭ kā′ tĭd/ *adj.* knowledgeable or worldly. *The young boy seemed sophisticated for his age.*

so•phis•ti•cat•ed² /sə fĭs′ tĭ kā′ tĭd/ *adj.* complicated enough to be appealing to those who have knowledge and experience. *The movie had very sophisticated special effects.*

spon•ta•ne•ous /spŏn tā′ nē əs/ *adj.* not planned or rehearsed. *After the play, the actors gave spontaneous answers to our questions.* —**spon•ta•ne•ous•ly** *adv.*

sprint¹ /sprĭnt/ *n.* a short footrace at top speed. *My favorite track event is the sprint.*

sprint² /sprĭnt/ *v.* **sprint•ed, sprint•ing, sprints.** to run at top speed for a short time. *I had to sprint to the bus stop because I was late.* —**sprint•er** *n.*

PRONUNCIATION KEY	
/ă/	pat
/ā/	pay
/â/	care
/ä/	father
/är/	far
/ĕ/	pet
/ē/	be
/ĭ/	pit
/ī/	pie
/îr/	pier
/ŏ/	mop
/ō/	toe
/ô/	paw, for
/oi/	noise
/ou/	out
/ŏŏ/	look
/ōō/	boot
/ŭ/	cut
/ûr/	urge
/th/	thin
/th/	this
/hw/	what
/zh/	vision
/ə/	about
	item
	pencil
	gallop
	circus
/ər/	butter

sump•tu•ous /sŭmp′ choo əs/ *adj.* very expensive and magnificent. *The king and queen gave a sumptuous banquet to celebrate their anniversary.* —**sump•tu•ous•ly** *adv.* —**sump•tu•ous•ness** *n.*

sump•tu•ous•ness /sŭmp′ choo əs nəs/ *n.* magnificence. *The weary traveler admired the sumptuousness of his hotel room.*

su•perb /soo pûrb′/ *adj.* excellent; very fine; first rate. *Our school orchestra gave a superb performance at the assembly.* —**su•perb•ly** *adv.* —**su•perb•ness** *n.*

sup•ple•ment¹ /sŭp′ lə mĕnt/ *v.* **sup•ple•ment•ed, sup•ple•ment•ing, sup•ple•ments.** to add to in order to improve or make more complete. *I like to supplement my lunch with a piece of fruit.*

sup•ple•ment² /sŭp′ lə mənt/ *n.* something that is added in order to improve or make more complete. *The latest sports magazine has included a supplement about exercise.*

sup•pose¹ /sə pōz′/ *v.* **sup•posed, sup•pos•ing, sup•pos•es.** to assume that something is true, especially for the sake of argument. *Just suppose that anyone could buy a ticket to visit the moon.* —**sup•pos•ed•ly** *adv.*

sup•pose² /sə pōz′/ *v.* **sup•posed, sup•pos•ing, sup•pos•es.** to think something is probable. *I suppose that I can go swimming on Saturday.* —**sup•pos•ed•ly** *adv.*

sus•pend¹ /sə spĕnd′/ *v.* **sus•pend•ed, sus•pend•ing, sus•pends.** to hang. *We suspended the birdfeeder from a tree branch.* —**sus•pen•sion** *n.*

sus•pend² /sə spĕnd′/ *v.* **sus•pend•ed, sus•pend•ing, sus•pends.** to support or hold in place as if attached from above. *The skilled operator could suspend the hot air balloon in the sky.* —**sus•pen•sion** *n.*

syl•lab•i•cate /sĭ lăb′ ĭ kāt′/ *v.* **syl•lab•i•cat•ed, syl•lab•i•cat•ing, syl•lab•i•cates.** to form or break into syllables. *For review, the students will syllabicate their vocabulary words.*

syl•la•ble /sĭl′ ə bəl/ *n.* a single uninterrupted sound that is a word or part of a word. *I divided the long word into syllables.*

T

tech•ni•cian /tĕk nĭsh′ ən/ *n.* someone who performs work requiring particular skills or techniques. *The dental technician cleaned my teeth.*

tes•ti•fy /tĕs′ tə fī′/ *v.* **tes•ti•fied, tes•ti•fy•ing, tes•ti•fies.** to make a statement of fact under oath in court. *A witness will testify that he saw the truck hit the car.* —**tes•ti•fi•er** *n.*

tes•ti•mo•ny /tĕs′ tə mō′ nē/ *n., pl.* **tes•ti•mo•nies.** a statement made under oath by a witness. *The jurors listened carefully to each testimony.*

trac•tion /trăk′ shən/ *n.* the friction, or grip, between a moving object and the surface over which it moves. *A mountain climber must have traction on the side of a cliff in order not to fall.*

trail¹ /trāl/ *v.* **trailed, trail•ing, trails.** to follow or lag behind; to be behind. *The old dog trails behind its owner.*

trail² /trāl/ *n.* a path or track through something like a forest. *We followed a trail on our hike through the forest.*

trans•ac•tion /trăn săk′ shən *or* trăn zăk′ shən/ *n.* the act of conducting or carrying out a business matter. *Banks keep records of their transactions.*

trans•fer¹ /trăns fûr′ *or* trăns′ fər/ *v.* **trans•ferred, trans•fer•ring, trans•fers.** to move from one person, place, or thing to another. *Please transfer your workbooks from your desks to the shelves.* —**trans•fer•a•ble** *or* **trans•fer•ra•ble** *adj.* —**trans•fer•a•bil•i•ty** *n.* —**trans•fer•rer** *n.*

trans•fer² /trăns′ fər/ *n.* the movement of something from one person, place, or thing to another. *The transfer of the puppy from its mother to our house went smoothly.*

trans•mit /trăns mĭt′ *or* trănz mĭt′/ *v.* **trans•mit•ted, trans•mit•ting, trans•mits.** to send or pass from one person or place to another. *Please transmit the message to me on my mobile telephone.* —**trans•mit•ta•ble** *adj.* —**trans•mis•sion** *n.*

tri•bu•nal /trī byoo′ nəl *or* trī byoo′ nəl/ *n.* a court of justice. *It took several days for the tribunal to hear from all of the witnesses.*

ty•rant /tī′ rənt/ *n.* a ruler who uses power cruelly, harshly, or unfairly. *The king was a tyrant who stole from his citizens.*

u•nique /yoo nēk′/ *adj.* being unlike any other. *The necklace my mother bought at a craft show is unique.* —**u•nique•ly** *adv.* —**u•nique•ness** *n.*

u•ni•son /yoo′ nĭ sən *or* yoo′ nĭ zən/ *n.* all together. *The class recited the poem in unison.*

u•nit[1] /yoo′ nĭt/ *n.* a person, thing, or group that is considered a part of a whole or larger group. *Our history textbook is divided into nine units.*

u•nit[2] /yoo′ nĭt/ *n.* a standard quantity or amount used for measurement. *An inch is a unit of length.*

u•ni•ty /yoo′ nĭ tē/ *n., pl.* **u•ni•ties.** the state of being as one; oneness. *The fans showed unity by cheering loudly for our team.*

u•ni•ver•sal /yoo′ nə vûr′ səl/ *adj.* related to all; worldwide. *Hunger is a universal concern.* —**u•ni•ver•sal•ly** *adv.*

var•i•a•ble /vâr′ ē ə bəl *or* văr′ ē ə bəl/ *adj.* not constant; changeable. *During the summer, my schedule for each day is variable.* —**var•i•a•bly** *adj.* —**var•i•a•bil•i•ty** *n.* —**var•i•a•ble•ness** *n.*

var•i•a•tion /vâr′ ē ā′ shən *or* văr′ ē ā′ shən/ *n.* the act or process of changing. *The doctor suggested a variation in his diet.* —**var•i•a•tion•al** *adj.*

va•ri•e•ty[1] /və rī′ ĭ tē/ *n., pl.* **va•ri•e•ties.** the state or quality of being varied or diverse. *Exercises that lack variety may become boring.*

va•ri•e•ty[2] /və rī′ ĭ tē/ *n., pl.* **va•ri•e•ties.** a collection of different things; an assortment. *I packed a variety of things for the trip.*

var•i•ous[1] /vâr′ ē əs *or* văr′ ē əs/ *adj.* of different kinds; different from one another. *Our class includes students of various backgrounds.* —**var•i•ous•ly** *adv.* —**var•i•ous•ness** *n.*

var•i•ous[2] /vâr′ ē əs *or* văr′ ē əs/ *adj.* several; many. *We visited various relatives during our trip.* —**var•i•ous•ly** *adv.* —**var•i•ous•ness** *n.*

veg•e•tar•i•an[1] /vĕj′ ĭ târ′ ē ən/ *adj.* made up of plants and plant products. *My vegetarian diet does not allow me to eat any meat.*

veg•e•tar•i•an[2] /vĕj′ ĭ târ′ ē ən/ *n.* a person who eats mostly plants and plant products. *The menu included dishes that vegetarians could eat.*

ver•sion[1] /vûr′ zhən *or* vûr′ shən/ *n.* a description or account given from a specific point of view. *My brother gave his version of how the lamp was broken.*

ver•sion[2] /vûr′ zhən *or* vûr′ shən/ *n.* a different form or variation of something. *In science class, we built a new version of a simple machine.*

ver•sion[3] /vûr′ zhən *or* vûr′ shən/ *n.* an adaptation of something such as a work of literature or art into another form. *I didn't like the movie version of the book.*

vin•dic•tive /vĭn dĭk′ tĭv/ *adj.* having or showing a desire for revenge. *The vindictive act didn't make anyone feel any better.* —**vin•dic•tive•ly** *adv.* —**vin•dic•tive•ness** *n.*

vir•tue /vûr′ choo/ *n.* a good or moral quality or trait. *Her greatest virtue is her kindness.*

vir•tu•ous /vûr′ choo əs/ *adj.* having or showing a good or moral quality or trait. *He was admired for his virtuous personality.*

vo•ra•cious[1] /vô rā′ shəs/ *adj.* eating or wanting large amounts of food. *Because I skipped lunch, I had a voracious appetite by dinner.* —**vo•ra•cious•ly** *adv.* —**vo•ra•cious•ness** *n.*

vo•ra•cious[2] /vô rā′ shəs/ *adj.* not being able to
  be satisfied in some activity. *I am a voracious*
  reader of history books.
  —**vo•ra•cious•ly** *adv.*
  —**vo•ra•cious•ness** *n.*

—————————(W)—————————

wade /wād/ *v.* **wad•ed, wad•ing, wades.** to
  walk in or through water or something that
  makes walking difficult. *We waded through*
  the cold water to the shore.

Editorial Development: Cottage Communications

Design and Production: Bill SMITH STUDIO

Cover Illustration: Dave Cutler

Photo and Illustration Credits: Page 6, PhotoDisc; 28, 50, 72, Clipart.com; 94, PhotoDisc; 116, Clipart.com; 138, Nancy Crampton; 160, Bettmann/Corbis; 182, Houston Chronicle

Borders and Icons: Brock Waldron

Context Clues Strategies: Adapted from Camille Blachowicz and Peter J. Fisher. *Teaching Vocabulary in All Classrooms.* (2002). New Jersey: Merrill/Prentice Hall. p. 26

Printed in the United States of America   10 11 12 330 9 8 7